D1453820

Dedication

I dedicate this book to my neighbor, Ms. Theresa Bane. She is author of *The Encyclopedia of Vampire Mythology, Actual, Factual: Dracula, Haunted Historic Greensboro, Ghost Stories and Folklore of the Piedmont, North Carolina,* and *The Encyclopedia of Demons*. Over coffee one day, Theresa poured over my photographs and listened to what I had to say about them. "There is a second book in here for you. You should write up a proposal," she said. She then shared the name of her publisher with me, and the rest is now history! My heartfelt thank you, Theresa, for your help and encouragement. Stop by for coffee anytime!

Acknowledgments

I would like to thank my good friend, Ingebord Cibelli, for her encouragement and for her proofreading: Thanks, Inge! You are one in a million!

[Contents

[Introduction

A neighbor of mine, who happens to be the author of a number of books, suggested that I had enough information and more than enough photos to write a second book about vampires, demons and aliens. I found it unsettling on a number of levels. First, did I really want to give the evil ones all of that publicity? Secondly, it has been my experience that should I offend them in any way, retribution rides a very fast horse! However, I decided that perhaps this book is needed and after asking my Spirit Guides and asking Father in prayer, I sent my book proposal to Schiffer Publishing. This is when they threw me a curve!

"We already have books on the demon/vampire theme, would you consider writing on the subject of UFOs and aliens?" I agreed. Frankly, there is only a fine line of difference between the two.

This book will tell all of its readers the truth, as I know it. It will not be romanticized or glorified. After all, there is nothing romantic or glorious about a war, or in killing, abducting, or dying. I believe in the truth, even when it is upsetting. It is my prayer that all of the people who have promoted evil, or have taken pride in being bad, will read this book. Many books romanticize evil, such as vampirism, and make it seem exciting. You see, there is very little honor

A SILENT INVASION

The Truth About Aliens, Alien Abductions, and UFOs

Rev. Debra S. Marshall

Schiffer Publishing Ltd

4880 Lower Valley Road • Atglen, PA 19310

Copyright © 2014 by Debra Marshall
Library of Congress Control Number: 2014932791

Type set in Univers LT Std/Book Antiqua

ISBN: 978-0-7643-4609-5
Printed in China

Schiffer Books are available at special discounts for bulk purchases for sales promotions or premiums. Special editions, including personalized covers, corporate imprints, and excerpts can be created in large quantities for special needs. For more information contact the publisher:

Published by Schiffer Publishing, Ltd.
4880 Lower Valley Road
Atglen, PA 19310
Phone: (610) 593-1777; Fax: (610) 593-2002
E-mail: Info@schifferbooks.com

For the largest selection of fine reference books on this and related subjects, please visit our website at
www.schifferbooks.com.

We are always looking for people to write books on new and related subjects. If you have an idea for a book, please contact us at proposals@schifferbooks.com.

This book may be purchased from the publisher.
Please try your bookstore first.
You may write for a free catalog.

among those who would destroy the common good. The truth is that evil is often illogical and self defeating. Truth, while sometimes difficult to hear and deal with, tends to call forth in most of us the moral codes we have been taught, the logical way to proceed in a crisis, and if neither of those things are there, truth that comes from Heaven will comfort us, and our Spirit Guides are there to help us during such times.

Come journey with us, then, all you seekers of truth. Come down a path not so often followed, to awaken this part of your memory, to begin lifting the veil that you have been wearing for so long. This book is as true as I can make it; it is not a work of fiction, and it is not dramatized or romanticized in any way. The photos contained in this text all, with the exception of a few digital ones, have negatives to prove their authenticity. They have been enlarged, some have been cropped, and such things as contrast and light/dark balance and sharpness adjusted in order to make the subject easier to see. There will also be interpreted drawings by my own hand to guide you. Prepare yourselves. You are about to learn the truth regarding our heritage, and the truth regarding aliens and alien abductions on our planet.

Please, read this book and pass it on to others as you deem appropriate. May Father open our hearts and minds as we begin this part of our awakening.

CHAPTER ONE

A Tale of Two Planets

If you ask fifty people what their conception of Heaven is, you will get fifty different answers. Some of us are influenced by what we have been told by various churches. Some may be influenced by books that they have read. All of us have thought about this at some point in our lives and then laid these thoughts to rest simply by saying, "But none of us will know until we get there, until we die." Until now, I would agree with that statement. However, we are now in the "end times" of our planet; we have approximately 70-100 years left. This fact makes it important for all of us to begin awakening to the truth.

What truth is there? How could I possibly know the truth about anything? I am not a scientist, not a physicist, or an astronomer. No, but once I began talking with my Spirit Guides in Heaven, I was informed that I had a Sacred Contract to fulfill. Part of this contract was to help my fellow man to return home to Heaven via Spirit Releasement, which I talk about in my first book,

To Help Lost Souls Find Home. The other part of this contract says that I am to help my fellow man to awaken and to understand:

1. Who we are as a people,
2. Why we were sent so far away from our original home,
3. How to speak with our Father and our Spirit Guides,
4. To prepare us to speak on our own to Heaven, so that Father and our Spirit Guides can work with us and give us messages, strength, and hope in the troubled days ahead.

To begin, it is necessary to talk about our original home. It is located in the 5th dimension; we on Earth are in the third. Our planet Earth is called "Terra" by people in the 5th dimension. Our home, which most of us call "Heaven," is a planet much like Earth, but far more ancient. There, we call it "Parutia" (*pah-roo-tee-AH*), which means "beautiful world." For those of you who have read my first book, this may seem redundant, but please bear with me. Most of you are probably asking what on Earth does this have to do with aliens and UFOs? Far more than you might think! After all, our history and heritage are both intertwined with the UFO phenomena we experience now on Earth.

There is a movie called *The Martian Chronicles*. In the film, a man has his family with him and they are living in a small colony on Mars. The people who originally lived there have all died of epidemics that we brought to Mars inadvertently. This man tells his children that he is going to show them a real Martian. They pack a picnic and go to an area where there are canals of water. He tells them to look into the water, and they will see a Martian. You see, *they* were the aliens, but they were then—at the canal—Martians, living on Mars. A less than brilliant example, perhaps, but I hope it has made my point. We are aliens; we are all from some place else, even though we do not yet remember it.

We come from a planet that is the third planet from the sun. Our sun is a twin star, the third one in the constellation Cassiopeia. Because it is a twin star, two suns are seen in the day time. At certain times during the year, there is daylight both day and at night. Weather there is very temperate, and is warm most, if not all, of the time. There is a rainy season, rather than a snowy winter. Two moons are seen instead of one at night. There was a third one, but it was destroyed during a dispute with

another world. There, people are far more advanced technologically than we are on Earth. They have long distance space travel and can move inter-dimensionally as well. Most of the other worlds in the 5th dimension also have this capability.

Now, it is time to discuss the battle between good and evil. We tend to ignore it, or see it as a story told to keep us in line and to help us to become better people. The truth is that the battle between good and evil began for our people when Father was chosen to become our Father, to be brought into the physical world and to then bring all of us into the physical world as well. How is this possible? Allow me to explain at least in general terms, the hierarchy in Heaven. There is a Universal Father, or our Universal God. He appointed Father to be our Father and to bring us into the physical world. It was, of course, necessary to bring Father into the physical world first. During this process, a Post Induction Shift occurred, and his souls energy split unevenly. This left 60% of his soul's energy as Father. The other 40% seemed to embody much of the anger and evil that we all possess in varying amounts, but keep in control by all of the checks and balances of an ordered and healthy mind. This 40% of Father's soul declared that if Father was to be seen as "the light," he would call himself "The Darkness." Neither wanted to take the other one back, and The Darkness basically began to undermine everything Father did one way or the other. He possessed all of the genius and intelligence of our Father, but he did not possess a conscience or a normal impulse control. As soon as Father's children developed space travel, he left Parutia, and became the primary force of evil. He traveled far and wide, establishing colonies made up of people abducted from other worlds, especially from Parutia. He also gave rise to many groups of people, many children.

Understand, Father was brought into the physical world to be father to many people, which he could create to look any way he wished. The Angels he made very tall, blonde haired and blue eyed, with white wings—and they do have the ability to fly. The early ones had very large round eyes and a heart shaped face; the more recent ones have an appearance similar to our own, but with blonde hair and blue eyes. With some minor differences, on Parutia, we look very much as we do here.

The Darkness brought his children into the physical world. It was impossible to take that ability away from him, without taking Father's ability away as well. Not all of his children have been discovered yet, but it is obvious that he sought to create his children to be as unlike Parutians as possible. It is also true that many were created as a military for him to use at his will. It is of note that in spite of their different appearance outwardly, all of his children's souls came from the same place as Father's children. We all have what we would deem human souls. Father created Angeldom and he created mankind, humanoids, made in his own image. The Angels were a bit like our first law enforcement and our first army. The Darkness created many different types of children and he gave them homes in many remote places throughout the universe. I will give you a partial list of his offspring, as they play a prominent role in our UFO sightings and in our alien abductions here on Earth.

The Darkside

The oldest known group were called "The Darkside." They were perhaps four feet tall, stocky, with faces that had a pig-like appearance. They wore dread locks (which were part of a headpiece) and heavy armor that looked a bit like that of a Samurai, and a bit like the alien in the movie "Predator." They were taken out during a fight approximately fifteen years ago. I have not been told which of his offspring were created next. I do not know the order in which they were created.

The Bru-Hoi

The Bru-Hoi, or "Brave Warriors," were a group who were slight in frame, four feet tall, with gray skin and the large almond-shaped black eyes, the same as the "Roswell alien." They had, I am told, very weak backs and thin bones, which has proven to be a hardship for them. They prided themselves on their intellect and on their lack of emotion. The truth is that they were not created totally without emotion, but they had to learn to control it from birth.

It bears repeating that all of the offspring of Father and The Darkness came from the same place. That is, their souls all came from the same place as our own. There were many different groups similar to the Bru-Hoi, with slightly different names.

The Bru-Hyashi

The Bru-Hyashi, or "Brave Army," were one such group. They lived in the same galaxy as Parutia and in many other galaxies scattered across the universe.

The Val Gorin

The Val Gorin, or "Valiant Lizards," lived on a planet which orbited the third star in Orion's Belt.

The Val Gorin-Sekah

One other group, The Val Gorin-Sekah, lived on a planet in the Cassiopeia constellation, but a great distance from Parutia. Sekah means "second command," because they did not wish to fight and wanted to live a peaceful existence. Therefore, they would not be called first to fight. They were crocodilian in appearance, with a snout and scaly skin. They had a very strong, muscular body without a tail. They had scales, I am told, but their bodies resembled ours except for that. They talked as we do, but with some hissing.

The Zan-Besii

The next group is called The Zan-Besii, or "Fierce Lizards." They walk upright as we do, have scaly skin, and talk with a hiss as do the Val Gorin. They are very much alike, except the Zan-Besii do not have a snout, but a more human-like profile. Their eyes, I am told, have a slit pupil, whereas the Val Gorin have round ones.

Druxsella 7.0

All of The Darkness' children were trained and encouraged to be very disciplined, militaristic, and not to show emotions as we do. As far as I am aware, many of the children of The Darkness have perished in wars or from the Druxsella 7.0 virus that has decimated over 1,200 planets thus far. For those of you who have yet to read my first book, this was listed as one of our planet's emergencies that we needed to be aware of. It is a genetically modified virus that is extremely lethal, and spread by all vectors.

In the beginning, the only way to tell if a person had this virus, and not an ordinary Druxsella virus, was to examine the virus. It should be positive for human cell marker 36b. This virus was first conceived as a doomsday weapon, and it lived up to that description. It caused madness, which led to complete organ system failure and death. By the end, those who suffered from this were not able to close their eye lids, and eventually could not sleep, talk, or swallow.

It is highly likely that this virus will eventually find its way to Earth, in fact, it is almost a certainty at this point, and Father wants us to be ready to isolate and test those suspected of having it. This knowledge does have a bearing on our UFO and abduction experiences here, as infected and mentally impaired people can make poor decisions, including sending warships our way because they can no longer understand that we pose no threat to them, as we are far behind them technologically.

One good example is our aging orbiting-waste-of-tax-dollars: our "space station." The one we have left manned by scientists with no completely reliable way to return home, having retired our space shuttles, which would normally be used to resupply them. The station has concerned any number of worlds, because to them, it implies that we now have developed distance space travel, and could be a threat to them in the 5th dimension. We are still a very long way from true distance travel, so it is hard to explain why we would even build a "space station" when we have yet to develop travel! This is, after all, like building a gas station before the invention of the wheel. Our people are at great risk of an attack by those on worlds who feel justified in destroying this floating lab, because they see it as some kind of military installation. To their way of thinking, if ships do not come and go, then why have it, unless it has defense capabilities? This is how it is perceived in the 5th dimension. Even amongst so many mentally impaired people universe wide, having a "space station" without distance travel simply makes no sense. Thus far, Father has protected us from such an attack. The truth that Father wants you to understand is that this station is aging and unsafe and is drawing a lot of attention from various worlds, some of which are impaired by the infection I have spoken of, and thus are more likely to attack us militarily.

The Spiritu Morte

Now it is time to discuss those children who were created both surgically, genetically, and biochemically. It is a safe bet that we do not know of all of them yet, but this brings us to the list of those we do know about. In The Darkness' Army, the foot soldiers would most likely be the Demons, or the Jinn. They are out-of-body human souls who have been altered energetically to look very frightening. I am told that greater than ninety percent of the Demons have turned themselves in to Father, following the demise of The Darkness several years ago, but the rest are still active here on Earth, and other worlds as well. The Generals in this army would be the Spiritu Morte or "Death Spirits."

They are out-of-body also. This fact is important, as it limits what they can do to the living. They appear as a skeleton in a black-hooded robe, often with a black snake (their tongue) moving in and out of their eye sockets.

The Valdurii

This takes us now to those who were created, not born. The Valdurii are the most feared of his army and are considered an elite killing force. They are human beings whose human bodies have been altered biologically, surgically, chemically, and genetically. It is of note that most, if not all, of them were forced into this role, without a clear understanding of what they would look like or how they would have to exist. There are seven known types of Valdurii.

Valduri Batuii *(Baah-too-ee)*

Valduri Batuii, or "Valiant Bats," are seven to ten feet tall and wear a very tough suit of armor, which leaves only the face exposed. They have bat-like wings and their armor has a tail attached to it, to make them seem more devil like. The process has darkened their skin, sometimes completely black, sometimes brown. In one rare case, a number of them turned purple. A few of them turned green. It has left them with the vulnerability of having to wear the uniform always, they cannot disrobe without fear of injury, which would be fatal to them. They may have to change armor when it wears out, but they cannot bathe, eat, or sleep as men do. Their eyes have been seen as red, and are sometimes visible without the rest of them being seen. I have had the experience of seeing them in this way. I have also felt their compactness, when one night I sat on the side of my bed, and extended my arms to stretch and yawn. As I did, my left fist hit something standing beside me with a thump! His torso felt like compacted straw—very compact. He was unseen by me, but I certainly could feel his presence. Needless to say, I yelled (Internally) for my Spirit Guides and Guardians to help me out of that one! Because I am allowed to do a type of casting out, and because I seek to do Father's bidding, I am often observed by these men. It helps to understand that they are human souls inside those blackened bodies, and that they are not terribly happy with the life that was thrust upon them. They can shrink down and enter a human body to feed on blood, but are not required to feed, in order to survive. (The Valduri Lupei is the same, but has a hood that resembles a wolf that he pulls over his face, and some have a wolf-like tail, others do not. They do not have wings.)

Valduri Loratu

Valduri Loratu, or "Valiant Bridge Hanger" spends much of his time hanging from trees in the woods. They are the same as the other Valdurii, but they do not have wings and they have a large cape with an uneven hem, a nod to bat wings, and they have bands on their wrists that the cape attaches to, if they wish to give the appearance of wings unfurled. What their exact function is I do not know, but I suspect observation is one function. They, too, are vampires, but neither has to feed to survive.

Valduri Gorin

Next, we have the **Valduri Gorin** or "Valiant Lizard." Their faces resemble the Val Gorin race, It is believed by Father that they

are Val Gorin who were forcibly volunteered into this role. They, too, are blackened by the process, and they do not have wings, but wear a cape. The Valduri Karnak have just recently been discovered. They have a face that has been altered to appear bug-like or scarab-like with a proboscis instead of a mouth. They do not have wings, either.

Valduri Skelatti

The **Valduri Skelatti** appear to be animated skeletons. All flesh has been removed, with blackened organs visible, beneath bone. They wear a cape. They have blood-red eyes. Their organs are held in place by a clear band worn around the body to hold their organs in place. Some have lost their organs and are animated skeletons, still carrying a human soul, some how.

Valduri Corpus Void

The last category of Valduri has been labeled **Valduri Corpus Void**. These poor souls were basically kidnapped and forced to undergo the chemical process, by people who did not know what they were doing. Consequently, their flesh has begun to rot, and the stench is overpowering. Anyone who says they smell rotting flesh during a haunting most likely has them near by. (It is also possible that this is the process used to create a Valduri Skelatti, but this is not yet known.)

The chemical process and biological process used leaves the Valduri with the stench of gangrene, and it is this biological and chemical mixture that turns their skins so black. The Valduri lives and yet they don't, not in the usual sense. They have no pulse, no bio-chemical activity at all. They can travel via the inter-dimensional corridors, without their physical bodies vanishing as it would with a live person. They can only feed on blood, but they are not required to feed at all. They do so usually by implanting themselves inside a host, and the host almost always dies from the process, due to a powerful bacteria-virus mixture, which is used in their own creation. This mixture rapidly destroys the red blood cells of the infected person. **If any of the Valduri are found lifeless, it is very important not to touch them!** Great care must be used in handling any such remains! Double gloves and masks would be in order, and perhaps isolation gowns also.

If ordered to frenzy, the Valduri cannot resist an order, and they can frenzy in large numbers. They must implant themselves inside the host. They do this by shrinking down to a size small enough to enter. The victim is almost always female. The Darkness often genetically and biochemically tied the frenzying behavior to sexual appetite and sexual desire. The Valduri are seven to ten feet tall—the normal height of males in that dimension. It is not understood how they shrink down at will.

The Valduri have been called such names as "the Mothman," "The Leeds Devil," "Gargoyles"—and they have been depicted as "The Bat-Winged Ones," as well. I am certain other names for them exist. They carry a lancet to open an area to drink from. They also prefer to inject their victim with a powerful neurotoxic agent similar to Curare, so they cannot thrash around, which could hurt the Valduri. Anyone who survives this can develop a systemic infection which is characterized by patches of gangrene developing on their organs and skin, which is eventually fatal and is infectious to others.

The Sleveless Signat: There are other children of The Darkness who are true Vampires, in the classical sense. They are living and have to drink blood to live. They cannot eat or drink anything else, except small sips of water. This has meant that they have had to wander about, world to world, to find humans to feed upon. Staying in one place has meant that the people who they feed upon begin to die out, having been so depleted for too long. They are called The "Slevessii Selvii," and another group is called "The Sleveless Signat." They have some differences in appearance. The Slevessii Selvii are about three feet tall, white skin, black to brown hair, and the men wear a goatee. The sclera of their eyes are very dark, nearly black. Their eyes, I am told, work the same way as ours, just the pigmentation is different. I have seen them depicted in any number of haunting accounts. The second group, the Sleveless Signat, have red eyes, and are clean shaven. They have a more troll-like appearance. I could readily see them as being called the Wee people of Irish lore.

The Doobisee is another group that is nearly impossible to describe. They are true shape-sifters, and are very intelligent and quick. Before being altered surgically and genetically by The Darkness, they existed happily in the wild, human souls who fed off of vegetation and hurt no one. This is perhaps the only human group who could claim that distinction. The Darkness turned them into true vampires, who can only drink blood, and they cannot tolerate the blood of animals for very long or they perish. Therefore, they have to feed off of human blood. Able to shape-shift to camouflage themselves against the trunks of trees, they can blend in, amazingly. They can also appear to be dogs, cats, or other small animals at will. The Doobisee can shrink down and go within the body of a human host to feed. They can go between sub-dimensions and, therefore, remain invisible to us, even when they are coming inside us. Since being altered, they appear physically to be a cross between a bat, a stingray, and a horse shoe crab.

Our Beginnings

To understand the UFO and alien problem, it helps to understand our early beginnings. We are, after all, aliens ourselves!

We have spoken of where we come from, and of how The Darkness and our Father came to be. We also have talked about The Darkness' offspring and we will also discuss their role in UFOs and the abductions that have taken place since men began inhabiting this planet.

Father is with us in the physical world of Parutia, in the 5th dimension. He decided to begin a colony of his children, some where else, some where remote. Why would we need a colony? Well, the reason was two-fold. Firstly, he wanted us to reincarnate, to live multiple lives and to learn from them, to hasten our spiritual growth. Secondly, he felt that it would be a good idea to have a place to escape to, if Parutia was rendered unlivable by The Darkness.

The first attempt to colonize Terra (Earth) was called Atlantis. It was in Southern France, near a rather large lake. I am told that it was like a frontier town in the American West and was comprised of clap-board houses and dirt streets. We were a small group of adults. I am told that I was one of the youngest there at 16 years of age. I had a dry goods store! We were all aware of who we were and where we came from. There were no children and we had to agree not to try. We signed up for two-year cycles, after which we would return home and others would take our place.

However, enter Satan, or Satani (*Say-Tahn-ee*), as he is called back home. He had just been exiled from Parutia and he and his followers came, begging for kindness, asking to stay with us. They gradually sowed seeds of unrest and anger, jealousy amongst the colonists. We had explosives to be used in mining and road construction. Some how, we went to war against ourselves, and blew our colony up! Those who seek to find the lost colony should stop wasting their time. I am told that the crater caused by the blast filled with water from the large near by lake, and it is now known as the Mediterranean Sea.

All of us are now currently living in our second attempt to colonize Earth. Father sent a couple to begin a small colony, and to basically people the planet. Their names were not Adam and Eve. They were actually called the Elohim Gabriel and Suzanna-Kei. Gabriel was perhaps 18 years of age, as was Suzanna-Kei. They were very much in love and it was expected that he would choose to give up his angelhood to remain married to her upon their return. They alone were permitted to know of home. They were not allowed to tell their children of their roots. They were to simply tell their children that they came from the Heavens, and that our Father in Heaven made us, and we were to pray to him. Gabriel had to undergo surgery to have his wings removed, as no one but his wife would know his identity in Heaven. They had to build everything from scratch, and probably were in caves until they could build huts or houses. They were alone, so they had to know how to deliver their children and how to use herbs for medicines. They had to live off of the land. It was a grueling, hard life for them. They died and returned home at approximately 150 years of age.

Their children spread out and began to meet people from worlds who had been sent to our earth to establish colonies. Father was aware of some of them and had given permission to them. Earth was ruled as a Parutian territory. It was seen as a Parutian territory, because as far as anyone knew at the time, our colony of Atlantis had been the first claim. There had been a terrible war on Earth a long time before, and Earth had recovered and was once more a beautiful green world. Gabriel and Suzanna-Kei's children intermarried with these people from other worlds, which is why Earth is so biodiverse. The original couple settled again in Southern France, and their offspring were forced by war to eventually settle in the northern lands, in what is now Norway, Sweden, and that part of our world. This is the reason why so many from that area are very fair-skinned and very blonde-haired and blue eyed, because Gabriel was pale with platinum hair and very blue eyes and Suzanna-Kei was also blonde haired and blue eyed.

I have given you a lot of information, but what does all of this mean? What does this have to do with the alien abductions and the UFO encounters that seem to be happening with an ever-increasing frequency? As far as we can surmise from our records, the UFO sightings and abductions began in the 1600s. These sightings coincided with the disappearance of people from those areas, even though a direct connection to the sightings probably was not made at that time. The children of The Darkness and other peoples that he either ordered or persuaded took part in these abductions. Remember, back home nearly everyone, every group of people has the capability to travel to this dimension by space ship and back again. No doubt, though I cannot prove this, many of the people who have vanished are aspects of higher selves back home on Parutia who work closely with Father, and are older souls who have the potential to be a force for good in our world. This certainly includes any people whose higher selves on Parutia are Angels. If abductions were to be made, a list of those seen as possible enemies of The Darkness or any of his regimes would be targeted. Some would undergo brain washing and torture to break them in ways that would prevent them from ever coming forward to serve Father. However, most of those abducted did not make it back home at all.

Bru-Hoi

Woods at the mining colony.

Detail View Worker in Hard Hat standing on loading dock?

Worker with hard hat and shorts, unloading a mothership at mining colony

The sword in the middle of the image it is a Civil War imprint, but to the right, you can see a Bru-Hoi man in an environment suit, with a sword that is actually a stun-gun.

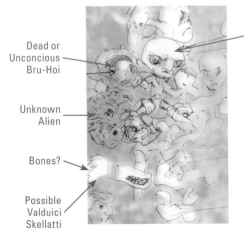

Bru-Hoi being arrested and restrained?

Dead or Unconcious Bru-Hoi

Unknown Alien

Hanover Co., VA Battle of Bloody Run

Bones?

Possible Valduici Skellatti

A Bru- Hoi being restrained.

Shuttle with hatch still open. Upper right: Three faces are visible from a window (two Leotyne— lion-like—and one Bru-Hyashi).

Large shuttle or mothership upper left, another lower right.

Original Full View

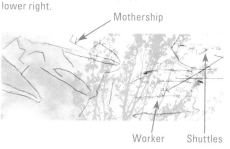

Mothership

Worker   Shuttles

Head of Pilot Visible

Close up of saucer crashing. Inverted colors show shape better. Note trail goes through trees, front more solid than back. This is another sub-dimension

Space Ship—small saucer about to crash. The saucer seems semi-transparent because it is in a sub-dimension other than our own.

Clouds are created to cover the vessels. The ship has 8 hatches open in the photo and are attached at each end to the other shuttles.

Another door and men standing there.

Three doors open.

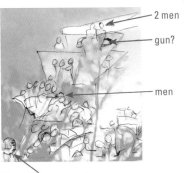

The sick or dead under yellow blanket being unloaded

Man in a gun turret?

2 men

gun?

men

Looks like a rectangle shuttle, not running?

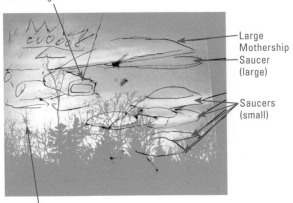

Large Mothership

Saucer (large)

Saucers (small)

Body from fight.

Round ship—mothership,
probably Regatta Morti (death ships)

Mothership and smaller shuttles. All of this is
around a mining colony.

Author has been told that this was a battleship over
her apartment—they were angry about her taking
photos.

Saucers
Large motherships
—possibly Regatta Morti
Small shuttle
Large Saucer Shuttle
5 smaller
saucers
(at least)
Small saucers

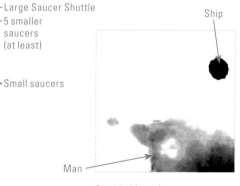

Ship
Man

Round ship and a man
committing suicide by jumping
from it (energy, author is told, is
very unhealthy for those aboard
the ships).

There are already a lot of saucers in the sky

Shuttle taking off. *Note insignia.*

Small saucers and Bru-Hoi

Sunset Scene showing a shuttle and saucer

Insignia as Shuttle takes off

Shuttle

Shuttle

One refueling

Men

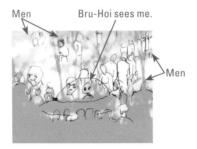

Men

Bru-Hoi sees me.

Men

One Bru-Hoi in small saucer, many men, some in military uniforms at the colony.

Silhouette of saucer detail

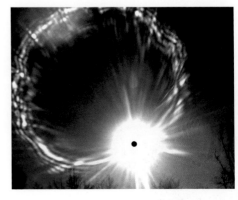

Two shots of a round ship in front of the sun with an energy halo.

Android

Bru-Hyashi.

Mothership Unloading. Five to Six people are visible from upper right, middle, and lower hatches.

Console

Bru-Hyashi

Robot

Bru-Hyashi?

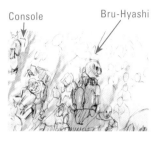

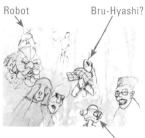

Robot

Bru-Hyashi looking over his shoulder. Others rushing about. Thick transparent stuff around trees is actually Doobisee forming a "privacy screen"; the grid they hang from is not visible.

Men

Zan Besii

Men

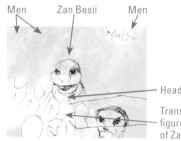

Head

Transparent figure in front of Zan Besii

Zan Besii, laughing at a social gathering. Mining colony or party or feast? Looks like a *Star Wars* Café scene. Many people around.

Zan Besii

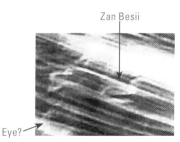

Val Gorin
"Valiant Lizard."

Eye?

The Zan-Besii in light tunnel, or energy vortex (same as inter dimensional corridor). He is in route to mining colony.

Val Gorin in uniform with insignia

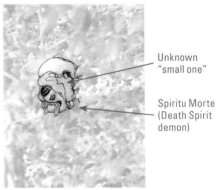

Unknown "small one"

Spiritu Morte (Death Spirit demon)

Original shot was from Wilderness Battlefield , Orange Co., VA. Note that the skull or "Spiritui Morte," lower left, is nearly out of frame.

Detail, Wilderness Battlefield, Virginia

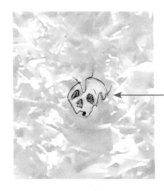

(Demon) Spiritu Morte hiding in leaves

Spiritu Morte

Wilderness Battlefield, Virginia

Valduri Lupei, one of the Bretheren.

Unknown man covered with Sandoolahs

Devil's Den, Gettysburg, Pennsylvania

Valduri Batui.

Detail of Valduri Lupei (Valiant Wolf) and small black clad figure beside him.

The wolf face is a hood/mask. These are human souls. The black figure and people are unknown.

CHAPTER TWO

Our Biodiversity Explained

The Rush To Colonize Earth

In my first book, I spoke in general terms about our biodiversity. After all, how could two young blue-eyed and blonde-haired people give birth to so many different genotypes? The answer of course is that would be impossible. But let me digress: Many years before Father was chosen to bring us into the physical world and establish his lineage, another group of people were living on our Earth. They were very technologically advanced. There were people on Mars and on Jupiter, as well. Mars had extensive tunnels where people lived during their coldest season; only the poorest had to survive their cold season above ground.

Jupiter had an experimental community that was under a protective bubble, as the harsh environment and the lack of breathable atmosphere made this essential. They were from Mars originally. Mars at that time had a breathable atmosphere very much like our Earth. War broke out, and within a fortnight, all three worlds were destroyed. The conflict first began in our Middle East, and spread outward. This was the epicenter. The atmospheres of Earth and Mars were destroyed and they were both nearly rendered scorched rocks. Anyone in Mars tunnels would no doubt be cooked alive by the heat of the nuclear fire storm. It is known that biological weapons were deployed as well. The Martian colony on Jupiter was also destroyed the same way.

Our Father was living on Earth at the time this war developed so very long ago. When he decided to begin a colony for us in another dimension, he chose Earth, as he had many fond memories of what Earth had been like before the war. Earth had recovered from our evil and was livable once more. Father helped to refurbish Earth and made it ready to be colonized. This is how we came to be here on Earth in the 3rd dimension.

Father left the Middle East area as desert, in hopes that no one would care to settle there. There is evidence now to suggest, per my Spirit Guides, that other worlds rushed in to mine minerals without Father's knowledge, even before our first colony attempt. When our first attempt failed and our "original couple" started another colony, other groups of people started colonies on Earth, following Father's example of simplicity. These colonies came without their technology, and were even instructed to worship idols and to do things that had characterized the early days of their planet and culture. It was considered an experiment. How would modern man react, and how would he evolve if stripped of his technology? Sadly, many of these worlds died due to wars with neighboring planets and some could not continue to finance their experiment. Those who had come to Earth found themselves stranded here.

The Draconians

The group who claimed the most land and had the largest colonies were the Draconians. These were the pyramid builders. They were people from worlds in the Draco (dragon) constellation. It is a little known fact that the Draconians were actually created by our Father. They settled the planet Draco, in the Draco constellation, after a disagreement with Father. The Draconians were humans like the Parutians, but with dark hair and eyes and olive complexions. On earth, we call them Hispanics, Mexicans, Egyptians, the Thai people, and most likely the Native Americans. They defected to the side of The Darkness, a move that I am told they later regretted. Some of them were surgically and genetically altered to have red skin and black hair and horns, which were surgically applied as a reward for good service. They wore goatees that were often shaved and stylized to look more devil-like. These were called "Luciferians."

It is suspected that there was another group that came into play in Egypt because Egyptian spirituality was foreign to the Draconians, and may have been borrowed from a group that was already in that area when they began their colony. The Aztecs held a coming of age ceremony for their male children. I am told that this is still practiced by Draconian groups in the

5th dimension. This would take place, I am told, when the child reached 16-19 years of age. They had to commit to memory and recite a passage of writing called "The Tasks of a Wise Man," which would be very similar to this:

The Tasks of the Wise Man
(Aztec) Bernardino Sahagun

The wise man: A light, a torch, a stout torch that
does not Smoke.

A perforated mirror, a mirror pierced on both
sides.

His are the black and the red ink, his are the
illustrated manuscripts,
he studies the illustrated manuscripts.
    He himself is writing and wisdom.

He is the path, the true way for others.

He directs people and things, he is a guide in
human affairs.

The wise man is careful (Like a Physician) and
preserves Tradition.

His is the handed-down wisdom; he teaches it; he
follows the path of truth.

Teacher of the truth, he never ceases to admonish.

He makes wise the countenances of others; to
them he gives
A face (a personality); he leads them to develop it.

He opens their ears; he enlightens them.

He is the teacher of guides, he shows them
their path.

One depends upon him.

He puts a mirror before others; he makes
them prudent, cautious, he causes a face; he
causes a face (a personality)
To appear in them.

He attends to things; he regulates their path, he arranges and commands.

He applies his light to the world.

He knows what is above us (and) in the region of the dead.

He is a serious man.

Everyone is comforted by him, corrected, taught.

Thanks to him, people humanize their will,
and receive a strict Education.

He comforts the heart, he comforts the people, he helps, gives Remedies, heals everyone.[1]

After reading this beautiful coming of age pledge, it is hard to put together in one's mind those who would value such a ceremony, and yet practice regularly human sacrifice. According to *The World's Religions* text:

> The old Toltec City of Teotihuacan, the abode of the Gods, some 30 miles to the North, and in its division into four quarters, it reflects the Aztec understanding of the cosmos...These four directions, together with the center, are the typical five directions of Central American (and of Chinese) cosmology.

You may recall that the Chinwazei (*n-WAH-zee*) or Asian people haled from a planet in the Draco Constellation, just as the Draconians did. Because there was peace between them, it isn't hard to think that perhaps they shared a common spirituality, or at least influenced each other's thinking on the subject. Once again, according to the text:

> The cosmos had it's axis or invisible center in the vertical line which ran through the city, with thirteen heavenly levels arranged above, and nine layers in the underworld. The number 5 was also important... the universe has five major periods, each ending with various calamities....We are now embarked on the period of the fifth Sun, when the sun rises in the East....But the universe is gravely unstable, for the continuation of order requires continuous sacrifices. Indeed, before the start of the fifth Sun, the gods had to combine to energize the sun, which did not rise above the horizon, by sacrificing themselves collectively. This myth provided justification for the continuing sacrificial cult which was centered in Tenochtitlan...So the Aztecs had this rather haunting and terrifying thought that indeed the sun might not rise tomorrow, that the onward harmony of the world was something which was forever in jeopardy...the sun required human blood: this was the ideology of human sacrifice, itself a great stimulus to warfare, which was waged to capture fodder for the gods...the central rites of the empire, presided over by the emperor himself, were human sacrifices in which a (human) victim's chest would be opened and the still quivering heart torn out and presented to the gods. It was a grim rite and may blind us to the beauty of the city itself, in its fertile valley amid lakes with towering mountains in view...its hanging gardens and intense cultivation of vegetables and fruits, its geometric layout, its white houses and great pyramidal temples...[2]

It is also stated in the same text that the Mayans believed that at the center of the cosmos stood the first tree. According to their sacred book, the *Popol Vuh*, the world tree is a magical tree from which springs the four sacred directions, as well as all of life. This all arises from the "sacred center," the point of all creation and provides the humans with access to all spiritual realms. (http://www.awareness.com/julaug07/ja07_mayan_world.htm).

At this time, there existed a race of people known as Aryans. They settled in what is now called India. There was a group of very peaceful people that were already there and they were conquered by the Aryans. A group of people known as the Nubians were from a planet called "Nubia" in the same solar system as Parutia (Heaven) in the 5th dimension. They settled in North Africa, in what is now called Ethiopia, and perhaps further south as well. They were dark skinned, but not as dark as some people from Africa who have skin with almost a dark violet undertone. It is thought, according to my Spirit Guides, that another group colonized South Africa and also what is now Australia. They became the Aborigines, but who they were before this has been lost in time. Another group from our own solar system in the 5th dimension settled in South Africa. They were a small group known as the Yah-Sah. They looked much like we do, with larger eyes, and a shorter build. Their spoken word included many glossal clicks. There are a number of tribes in South Africa today that speak with these clicks, which may be a carryover from intermarriage with the Yah-Sah. There was a planet, also in our solar system back home, called Scotlandia. The people called themselves Scotlandians. They settled in what is now the area of Scotland, although the borders were different back then. A group called the Gesholdistat (Gess-hol-dah-stad) settled in the area of what is now Ireland. They were close neighbors to the Scotlandians, in our solar system.

But what of the Native Americans? It is thought that the Native Americans were a combination of the Draconians and the Asian people who settled in places like China and Japan as well as some island natives. The Asians were people from a planet that was also in the Draco Constellation, but not the same one as the Draconians. They called themselves the Chinwazei (*Chin-WAH-zee*). Their planet was known as "Chin-wah-SAH-see."

It is uncertain how many of these colonies sprouted up before our first attempt to colonize Earth. It is highly possible that there were other groups that came and went or simply died off, unable to conceive. What was not understood by these groups at that time, was that we cannot go from our native dimension to another and be able to bear children. Why this is so, I do not know. I am told that in order to have children here, Father has had to place the soul of the child to be born into the fetus at the appropriate time. This was done for our own people and Father gave these other groups this information as well, so their colonies would have a chance to survive. However, many just didn't see why it was necessary and as a result, varied colonies died out.

Father began doing this for larger groups that our own people were intermarrying with, such as the Egyptians. Unfortunately, their Royals had tried to intermarry to keep their bloodline pure until they had many, many congenital birth defects. Tutankhamun was one example of this. King Tut was the second or third soul from Parutia to be placed into an Egyptian fetus, in order to help that country survive. By then, their native planet was gone, due to war. It is known that he walked with a cane, due to scoliosis, or curvature of the spine. It is also believed by my Spirit Guides that he would have developed Marfan's Disease or syndrome, of which his father Akhenaten was thought to be a sufferer. I am told that King Tut was only 10 or 11 years of age when he met with his fatal "hunting accident" with Eye. I am also told that he had undescended testicles and could not have fathered a royal heir. I am told further that he and his sister, though encouraged to sleep together (the custom by then), did not do so, and that King Tutankhamun was told by his father that he would not live to adulthood. He intended to carry on the faith of his father, which the High Priests were very much against. Akhenaten was not a Parutian soul, but one of the last to know who they were as a people and where they were originally from. It is not known, however, if there was already another group in that region with which they melded.

Full view of Valduri Loratu in a tree (circled).

Woods near mining colony.

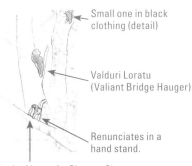

Small one in black clothing (detail)

Valduri Loratu (Valiant Bridge Hauger)

Renunciates in a hand stand.

Back of legs of a Slevess Signat (baby-like appearance)

Door

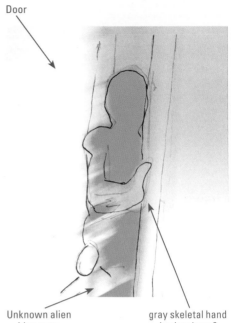

Valduri Loratui   Note: red-orange, black aura   Unknown alien   gray skeletal hand
                                                              —blue aura   —broken bone?

Detail of a bad fracture of
right arm of a Val. Loratu,
which looks as though
he tried to use wood and
screws to stabilize it.

Slevessi Selvee.

Unashamed People.
The face may be fuller and
rounder than this sketch.

Black Hair

Black eyes

White Skin

Wears white "Pajama"-type garb

Approximately 4 feet

True vampire

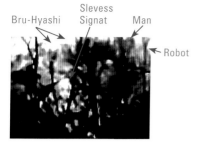

Slevess Signat.
This was at the mining colony.

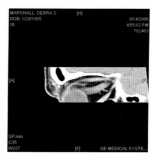

CT Scan auditory canal
—Doobisee and Slevess
Signat inside human host.

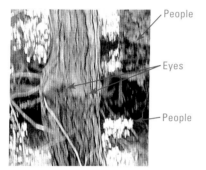

Doobisee near mining colony.

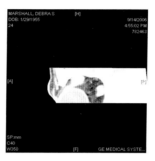

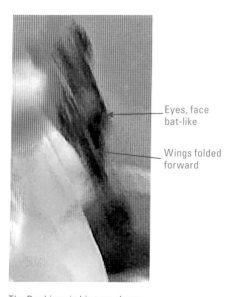

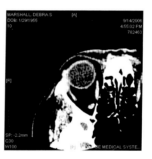

SalMartin elder; also Doobisee
in CT Scan during an attack.

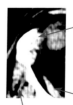

What's left of SalMartin
being eaten by Doolisee
and Sandoolahs (san-
doo-LAHS)

Left of hoof

Doobisee (true appearance)
lower left inside a human body
near the eye during CT scan.

The Doobisee in his true shape;
photo taken in author's home.
At bottom is his pup. Doobisee
are both male and female and
can conceive when conditions
are right.

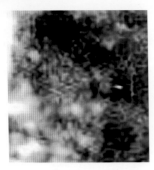

Sandoolahs and other small children of the Darkness. (Taken at Devil's Den, Gettysburg, PA.)

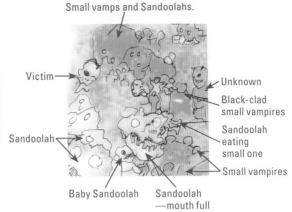

Small vamps and Sandoolahs.

Victim

Sandoolah

Unknown

Black-clad small vampires

Sandoolah eating small one

Small vampires

Baby Sandoolah

Sandoolah —mouth full

Note: Also have very bright eyes

Sandoolahs work together. They and other vampires have human souls.

Doobisee?

Sandoolahs have very bright eyes, and black ocotopus-like bodies that appear shaggy. They, like the Doobisee, can shape shift. (Taken at Devil's Den, Gettysburg, PA.)

CHAPTER THREE
The Nazca Lines and Other Signs

Upon our Earth, there are any number of sites that are a mystery to us. One such site is that of the Nazca lines. These mysterious drawings are located in the Peruvian desert, about 200 miles south of Lima. They are found on a desert plain that lies between the Inca and Nazca Valleys. This area is approximately 37 miles long and 1 mile wide. The Nazca lines were first discovered by Peruvian Archeologist Torbio Mejia Xessepe in 1927.

Science has broken the images formed by these lines into two categories. These are the biomorphs and the geoglyphs. The biomorphs, as the term suggests, are 70 animal and plant figures, including a spider, hummingbird, pelican, monkey, heron, condor, dog, parrot, iguana, whale, vulture, tree, flower, a set of hands, and a human figure. There are approximately 900 geoglyphs, including trapezoids, triangles, geometric shapes, straight lines, parallel lines, spirals, and circles.

Both the geoglyphs and the biomorphic shapes are drawn with a precision that is remarkable. The lines are very straight, for instance. The most defining characteristic, however, are their size. They are so large as to be indistinguishable from the ground. They must be seen from the air in order to see the images as a whole. The largest is the Pelican, which is 1,000 feet across. It was not until the 1930s, when an aircraft surveying the area for water, reported seeing them. The intersecting lines actually resemble a modern day airport.

A number of theories have been suggested as a possible explanation of their existence. Swiss writer Eric Von Daniken suggested that they were put there to give direction to ancient visitors from space. An American explorer by the name of Paul Kosok, when visiting the area in the 1940s, stated that they were used as an astronomical calendar of sorts. When he tested his theory by entering all of the data into a computer, however, it was found that the number of lines coinciding with astronomical events was no greater than chance. Tony Morrison, a British explorer, hypothesized that given a tradition of the indigenous people of the area to put religious shrines along straight pathways, he felt that this might actually be a complex network of pathways, by which the pilgrims would walk from shrine to shrine as part of a spiritual ceremony. There are other questions that beg to be answered:

- How were they built?

- How were they executed with such precision on so large a scale?

- How have they remained intact for so long a time?

It is thought that they have survived because this area is so very dry and windless. They appear to have been created by brushing away the red pebbles and dirt to reveal the white sandy soil beneath the surface. Writer Jim Woodmen believes that they had to be made with the help of someone in the air. However, once again, how could they have been working from the air at a time when the Nazca Indians would have been essentially in their stone age? Mr. Woodmen's hypothesis is that they constructed some sort of rudimentary hot air balloon in order to view it from the air. He constructed a hot air balloon from materials that they would have had and managed a flight, but for only two minutes—certainly not long enough to prove his theory. Other scientists believe that it was done using simple surveying techniques. Why? Why construct something you would never be able to see? Yet

another theory has been put forth by David Johnson and Steve Mabee. They believe that these lines relate to native aqueducts, pointing to underground water sources. This area is one of the driest on Earth, getting less than one inch of rain per year.

Another odd fact is that headless bodies have been found in that area, buried in the seated position. A total of eight bodies have been discovered, each with a ceramic jar next to them. Decorated with a picture of a head on each jar, the head showed a tree growing out of it, and eyes growing out of the tree. In an article in *Current Anthropology*, Christina Conlee of Texas State University states:

> Human sacrifice and decapitation were part of powerful rituals which would allay fears by invoking the ancestors to ensure fertility and the continuation of Nazca society. The decapitation of the La Tiza individual (La Tiza is the area in which it was found) appears to have been part of a ritual associated with ensuring agricultural fertility and the continuation of life and rebirth of the community.[3a]

It is impossible to know what became of their heads. However, it is known that the Nazca often took "trophy heads." They would remove the brain and soft tissue from the head, sew the lips closed with cactus spines, and drill a hole through the forehead to accommodate a rope for hanging. Even more disturbing is that these heads were not war trophies. DNA evidence shows that they were from the Nazca tribe! This suggests that the decapitations were done as part of a religious ceremony. According to the Neal A. Maxwell Institute for Religious Scholarship and an article written by Mr. Allen J. Christensen, 1997, the tree of life was a powerful symbol for the Mayas at that time. Sacred trees represented the power of life to spring forward from the underworld, where the Sacred Tree's roots were thought to exist. Ancient Mayan texts indicate that a great world tree was grown or was "erected" at the dawn of time to hold up the canopy of the sky. According to Quirigua Stela C, which is a large monument found in Eastern Quatamala, the act of the establishing of the Sacred Tree took place 13.0.0.0.0 4 Ahaw 8 Kumk'u or August 13, 3114 B.C. This was called "Lying-down-Sky, First-Three-Stone-Place," because it was there that the sky once lay unsupported against the Earth.[3b]

It is also worth noting that Phillis Pitluga, an astronomer at Adler Planetarium and Astronomy Museum, believes, based on computer-aided studies of star alignments, that the giant spider is an anamorphic diagram of the constellation Orion. She further suggests that three of the straight lines coming from this figure could be used to track the changing positions of the three stars in Orion's Belt[3c]. This information interests me, due to the fact that one branch of the Val Gorin came from a planet that orbited the third star in Orion's belt. A fair number of the Draconian people were aligned with The Darkness, and therefore may have had friendly relations with the children of The Darkness, including the Val Gorin.

The Chinwazei people were on friendly terms with the Draconians and probably the Darkness. They were, I am told, very well respected and liked by Parutia and many other planets and people, universe wide. The fact that the Draconians at Nazca were practicing human sacrifice, with head decapitation shows that they were practicing some very dark religious ceremonies. It had long been thought that The Draconian people—the Mayas and the Incas—had been influenced and acted upon by Satan and the Jinn to practice such rituals. According to my Spirit Guides, those who served The Darkness at that time are thought to have been divided into several categories according to the way in which they would be deployed in the event of war. The Spider referred to the Val Gorin, who lived on a planet orbiting the 3rd star in Orion's belt. If Ms. Pitluga is correct, then, the Nazca lines that seem to track the position of the three stars in Orion's belt would be used for determining a window or optimum time for their arrival or reentry, and a time for their departure, probably to conserve fuel and to shorten their voyage. This suggests that the Draconian colonies here—the Incans, Mayans and perhaps others—had a good working relationship with the Val Gorin and probably received supplies in exchange for things that they might have to sell. I am told that Earth was not considered Parutian territory at that time, so it is possible that they were selling mineral rights to other worlds.

The Chinwazei (*Chin-Wah-zei*) had colonies in areas that are present-day China, Korea, Japan,

Thailand, Viet Nam, and eventually a number of islands as well. It is possible that they intermarried with the Draconians in a number of areas, such as Thailand. The Nazca Lines, then, represent the first known space port of our Earth, which received ships from at least 3 different worlds. These would not be the mother ships, but smaller, lighter shuttle craft, and possibly supply drones.

But what of the symbols? I am told by my Spirit Guides that they were not made originally by hand. They were carved into the flat dry land by lasers from spacecraft. After that, the people of the area would need to periodically clear the red pebbles away and keep them visible. This does explain the precision of the lines, as well as the art work of animals and plants. It is worth noting that the Incas and Mayans both built pyramid structures and that the Draconians had such structures on their world as well. Therefore, this could be taken as evidence that the Egyptians, as well as the Incas, Mayans and the Thailanese, all had Draconian roots. It is also worth noting that the Draconians favored the use of the dragon in their art work, which is the symbol for the constellation Draco, their point of origin. The same can be said for the Chinwazei, who also haled from a planet in the Draco Constellation. It must also be noted that dragons were used to symbolize hallucinations during Mayan religious rituals. Perhaps this was also indicative of the rise of the Kundalini energy from the base of the sacrum to the crown during profound religious experiences. The Kundalini is often depicted as a serpent wrapped around our lower spine seven times.[4]

In an article in *National Geographic* magazine, an ancient city in Guatemala called Takalik Abaj is suspected of having served as a type of observatory. The site was first discovered by a late 19th century Botanist. The area is approximately 2.5 square miles or 6.5 square kilometers in size. It contains more than 1 dozen large plazas, 80 buildings, one of which held the trappings of a Mayan King. The city consists of 277 stone monuments from Olmec and later Mayan cultures. Indeed, the name "Takalik Abaj" means "Standing Stones." One Archeologist, Christa Schieber de Lavarreda, who is of the Guatemalan Ministry of Culture and Sport, has also excavated and investigated this site.

One large platform called "structure 7" appears to have served as an observatory. Ms. Christa Schieber de Lavarreda, along with Marion Popenae Hatch, and Miquel Orrego Corzo found that the alignment of the stones on this structure coincided with the constellation Draco—the Dragon. On structure 7, they discovered 660 vessels around the stela and deposits of ceremonial incense. Deep inside a small building in the back of the structure, was a royal grave of one of the last Mayan Kings.[5] On these stones, images of serpents or dragons are found, as well as an image of the head of a crocodile or perhaps a god who is half man and half crocodile. I believe that this suggests that the Val Gorin were trading and visiting with this group as well.

In their home dimension, the Draconians would have access to "tractor" beams that could easily be used to lift and place huge stones, such as those in the Mayan pyramids as well as in Egypt. This could easily be done from a ship orbiting Earth. Whether this was the case, however, may never be known. According to my Spirit Guides, it is known that the Draconians most likely merged and intermarried with another group of people who had already settled in what is now Egypt. However, their identity has been lost in time. Most, if not all, of these colonies were patterned after ours in that after the failure of Atlantis, no one was sent here in possession of their higher technology. They were told to live as their ancestors did many centuries before on their native planets. Therefore, after several generations living in very primitive conditions, most of the knowledge of who they were and where they were from would be lost. By that time, the contact they had at areas like Nazca would possibly be enshrouded in religious significance. Those men who arrived would have been seen as gods to the natives there.

The evidence of aliens coming to our planet exists apart from the Nazca Lines, as compelling as they are. There are those who propose that men from space visited Earth in ancient times and contributed to our development of technology. This supposes that man was put here and born here, as part of God's plan and are therefore truly of this planet. In other words, man is not an alien here. It has been suggested that this contact influenced the development of humankind, including our cultures and religions. Many also believe that the deities from our religions may actually be extraterrestrials.

There is an ancient cave painting found in Val Camonica, Italy. It is believed to have been painted around 10,000 BC. It depicts two human figures, with knees bent as if they are floating. They do appear to be wearing "bubble" type helmets, and really do look like astronauts.

Proponents of these beliefs often maintain that mankind itself has been fathered by such men and visitations represent their studying us and perhaps monitoring our progress. It is also commonly believed that these visitors built monuments, such as the pyramids of Egypt and the Moa stone heads of Easter Island.

Francis Crick, who co-discovered the double helix structure of DNA, strongly believed in the concept of "Panspermia," that is the seeding of life upon this planet. He talks at length about his theory in his book *Life Itself*. Further, Thomas Gold, a professor of Astronomy, has been said to suggest the "garbage theory" of the origin of life. In his theory, he says that life here may have arisen out of a pile of garbage or waste products dumped here by extraterrestrials a very long time ago. This to me is particularly insulting and very unlikely. Have any new life forms resulted from our fields of refuse? Not likely.

A man by the name of Zecharia Sitchin, author of the series *The Earth Chronicles*, interprets ancient Sumerian and Middle Eastern texts, megalithic sites, and artifacts from around the world. One of his theories suggests that the gods of ancient Mesopotamia were actually astronauts from the planet "Nibiru," which, he claims, the Sumerians believed to be a remote twelfth planet, counting the Sun, Moon, and Pluto as planets. According to my Spirit Guides, Nibiru was basically a large asteroid, the 12th body orbiting its sun in that solar system. This, of course, meant that it was a very cold place, without an atmosphere and the colonists lived under a bubble. Nibiru would also be associated with Marduk, an ancient god. According to Sitchin, Nibiru continues to orbit our sun, on a 3,600 year rotation. Sitchin also suggests that the asteroid belt between Mars and Jupiter is the shattered remains of the ancient planet "Tiamet," which he claims was destroyed in one of Nibiru's orbits through the solar system. Modern astronomy has found no evidence to support Sitchin's claims.

According to Sitchin, the Sumerians relate how 50 Anunnaki, the inhabitants of Nibiru, came to Earth approximately 400,000 years ago with the intent of mining raw minerals, especially gold, for transport back to Nibiru. With their small numbers, they soon wearied of the task and set out to genetically engineer laborers to work the mines. After much trial and error they eventually created Homo Sapiens, the "Adapta" (model man) or Adam of later mythology. Sitchin claims the Anunnaki were active in human affairs until their culture was destroyed by global catastrophes caused by the abrupt end of the last Ice Age, some 12,000 years ago.

Seeing that humans survived and all they had built was destroyed, the Anunnaki left Earth after giving humans the opportunity and means to govern themselves."[6]

Is there truth to what Sitchin maintained? According to my Spirit Guides, it is most probable that the asteroid belt between Mars and Jupiter is the result of one of Mars moons being destroyed during the war of long ago, that killed all of life on Earth and Mars, as well as a bubble or domed experimental colony on Jupiter. The moon was called "Tiamat." Once again, according to my Spirit Guides, Anunnaki is misspelled and mispronounced. It is "na-NU-kai" which means "legions of evil beings."

The name Marduk does not refer to a pagan god. It is the name of one of the fallen angels from long ago, who followed Satan to Earth. That the legions of evil ones were here extracting minerals while the ownership of our planet was being contested is not at all hard to believe.

Another thing that makes sense is the name "Nibiru." Nibiru was an illegal mining colony that no longer exists. It was destroyed during a war in what would be our 1700s, AD. Furthermore, no one from Parutia (Heaven) was here on Earth during the Ice Age. The dinosaurs were all being called home because of the unfavorable climate changes. According to my Spirit Guides, the dinosaurs still exist on Parutia, but are small reptiles! Why they grew so very, very large here on Earth is as yet unknown. They were sent here ahead of us as an experiment. Also of interest is the way they were called home. It was done in a very similar way to the movie *Jurassic Park*, in that they were created so that their bodies were unable to produce an enzyme. Father gave them this missing enzyme during their reign. When it was time to bring them back home, it was withheld. Why they grew to such size, however, will always remain a mystery.

But what of Nibiru and the Nanukai? It is our belief that the legions of evil ones were using Earth as their laboratory for genetic experimentation, and they were most likely taking numbers of colonists with them, to enslave them and to force them to work in the mines of Nibiru.

My Spirit Guides inform me that the Sumerians were originally a "Yah-Sah" colony. The Yah-Sah were not children of Father, but they were very friendly with Father. They looked like us, but they had larger eyes, and smaller hands. When I spoke of them before, you might recall that they also had a colony in South Africa and that they spoke with a type of glossal click. It is known that the Nanukai moved in and shared, or perhaps more likely took over, the Sumerian colony. They were not just fallen angels, but other humans as well who served evil (The Darkness), which the Sumerians did not. The abrupt end to their involvement came as a result of the Sumerians, who forcefully ejected this group of evil people from their colony, possibly by burning it down, so there would not be anything left of value to attract them. I am told that most of the Yah-Sah were killed in this uprising as well.

I find the account by Mr. Sitchin to be interesting in another way also. It would be just like the Jinn or the fallen ones to brag about the incident and to say that they had fostered and taught the colonists everything— even how to govern themselves!

In summary, I would have to say many people have given the existence of "Ancient Astronauts" much thought and have put forth many interesting theories and have offered as evidence the architecture and artistry of many primitive cultures. The one thing, and perhaps the most important piece of the puzzle that they seem to be unable or unwilling to entertain, is that we are, all of us, aliens or visitors to this world. We are the second colonization attempt of volunteers from our home land of Parutia or Heaven, if you prefer. However, many other people from many other far-off places colonized this world at different times. Before and during the Ice Age, we were not here—only the dinosaurs. However, it is not at all impossible that other people from other worlds were and much of the evidence presented as proof of ancient astronauts would seem to suggest this is so.

We have spoken about the pyramids of Egypt and the Mayans, and that it would have been much easier to build them with the help of "tractor" beams to help lift and place the huge blocks of stone. The stone could have been cut this way, also. This could be true of Stonehenge in England, but this theory is arguable. There is a very ancient method of raising stones called "The Herodotus Machine," which has recently been shown to work on stones the size of Stonehenge. I am told by my Spirit Guides that the Moa statues of Easter Island were cut and placed by sheer manpower, and perhaps by a method similar to the Herodotus method. The people, who are known as the Resilva, placed these statues without the help of the space ships that brought them to our world. These statues represent the founding Fathers of their colony, and were placed as if looking out to sea. They were placed in a way so as to greet visitors to Easter Island. Unfortunately, the wrong visitors came. I am told that their island, their colony, was immediately attacked by Satan and his men. Everything of value was taken and they lived a barren and difficult life until the death of their colony, a year or two later. When they were dropped off, it was with the understanding that supply ships would come, but none came. They were not aware that a war had taken place in the interim.

I am told that they built ships and occasionally made trips to near by Galapagos Island, but other than that, they lived a very difficult and lonely existence. I am told, also, that they were very good, very decent people who deserved better. According to my Spirit Guides, towards the end of the colony, they lived much of the year underground in the lava tubes. This was done to avoid people who came to the island, perhaps to avoid an attack.

I am also told that they were sent here without weapons. They were pacifists who did not believe in fighting. No doubt, by the end of the colony, they had most likely learned how to make primitive weapons, and had become expert fishermen. This information has been given to me by the Resilva, themselves. Father and my Spirit Guides allowed this communication so that their story could be told. According to the leader of the Resilva colony on Parutia, they lived underground much of the year due to the climate. They were not accustomed to our atmosphere, which had less oxygen than their world and it was also "hellishly hot and very humid, making breathing difficult."

Their name "The Resilva" means "Stalward Ones." At that time, Easter Island consisted of two islands with a channel of water in between. They lived on the island now referred to as "Poike."

It is worthy of note that there have been any number of people who believe that aliens have abducted them to give them a message to bring back to their own people. The book *Communion* is one such account, written by author Whitley Strieber. Since the 1950s, many religious sects or cults have appeared. The Aetherius Society, Church of the Sub-Genius, Heaven's Gate, Industrial Church of the new World Comforter, Raelism, Scientology, Unarius Academy of Science, and Universe people, to name a few. UFO Religion refers to a religion that equates UFO occupants with gods, or other semi-divine beings. They usually describe the beings as possessing a higher degree of technology and often they are observing and trying to help or educate our people here on Earth. Also, in many of these faiths, the aliens wish to prepare mankind for their journey home, to help us to be worthy of the next step of our journey. These religions have predominately begun in more highly developed countries, such as the United States, Canada, France, and the United Kingdom. Perhaps this is so, as more education tends to open the mind and less superstition gives us the license to suppose things beyond our present reality.

Aetherius Society

The Aetherius Society was founded in 1950, by George King. Mr. King claimed to have been contacted telepathically by an alien named Aetherius who spoke for an Interplanetary Parliament. According to the members of this group, their society acts as a vehicle for information from Aetherius or other cosmic beings, so that these messages can be spread to the rest of us, here on Earth. He received these messages telepathically during meditation. According to my Spirit Guides, Mr. King was indeed receiving these messages from an actual person from another world during his meditation, but it is unknown who this person was. They, my Spirit Guides, tell me that Aetherius was not one of Mr. King's Spirit Guides.[7]

The Church of the Sub-Genius

That leads us to The Church of the Sub-Genius, which was founded by Ivan Stang and Philo Drummond. It began with the publication of the pamphlet "Sub Genius Pamphlet #1." It is known as a Parody Religion due to its frequent use of humor and comedy. It has over 10,000 members worldwide. For $30, a person can become "An Ordained Sub Genius Minister." This group, I am told, has embraced many atheist and agnostic groups. The church prophesied that its founder, J.R. Dobbs, was in contact with an extraterrestrial race called "The Xists," who were scheduled to launch a world-wide invasion of Earth on July 5, 1998. The expected day came and went. The group now holds an "X-Day" celebration yearly on July 5th. According to my Spirit Guides, these men are hardcore agnostics who founded their church, in my opinion, with tongue planted firmly in cheek.[8]

Heaven's Gate

The next group is that of Heaven's Gate. In 1997, one of its founders convinced thirty-eight followers to commit mass suicide. They believed themselves to be aliens who were awaiting a spaceship that would arrive with the comet Hale-Bopp. They believed that they had to die in order for the space ship to transport them home to Heaven. I am told by my Spirit Guides that one of their leaders, Mr. Applegate, was very happy to get home and to discover that Father does exist! Apparently, they ran (out of fear and confusion) from their Guardians and then began to wander in search of help. It is true that we do have to leave our physical bodies to return home via the "light" or inter-dimensional corridor. Ships could be used to take us home, as we do have inter-dimensional travel. However, this would not be practical because there are too many of us going home daily to make it feasible. What stands out the most to me is that during the time that Hale-Bopp comet passed Earth, I was working on a farm as a nurse/home health aide. While at work one evening, I spoke with the members of Heaven's Gate and helped them home.[9]

That summer was, for me, absolutely one of the strangest and most surreal times of my life! I was just learning how to help souls to return home, and for a short while, the Hale-Bopp comet hung in our sky, visible even during the day. It was like a picture someone had placed there. It was also the time of many lessons for me, which I will discuss later in this book.

The Industrial Church of the New World Comforter

The Industrial Church of the New World Comforter was founded by Allen Michael in 1973. However, in 1947, Allen Noonan, who was a sign painter in Long Beach, California, claimed that he had a telepathic encounter with a UFO. He then changed his name to Allen Michael (changed because he was told that he was an aspect of Archangel Michael).

In 1954, he claimed to have had a physical encounter with a flying saucer at Giant Rock, in the Mojave Desert of California. During the "summer of love," he became vegan. He opened a Vegan Restaurant at the corner of NE Height and Scott Streets in San Francisco, called "The Here and Now." His group, called The One World Family, lived in two communal houses during the late sixties and early seventies in Berkeley, California. His vegan restaurant later moved to a larger building and it was then called "One World Family Natural Food Center." He published a cook book called *Cosmic Cookery*.

His vision for his new world order changed during that time, as he painted a mural in his restaurant of a farmer holding a pitchfork, a worker holding a hammer, and a soldier holding a gun. They had their arms around each others shoulders, and off in the distance in the sky were three flying saucers. The title reads *Farmers, Workers, Soldiers – Revolution by 1976!* Allan Michael founded The Industrial Church of the New World Comforter in 1973. He published the first volume of his revelations, *The Everlasting Gospel*, in 1975. The group and the restaurant relocated to Stockton, California, and Allen Noonan ran for President of the United States in the 1980 and 1984 elections on the Utopian Synthesis Party ticket.[10]

The Nation of Islam

The next of the five remaining groups that we will discuss is called The Nation of Islam (not to be confused with the traditional faith of Islam). which subscribes to the belief that UFOs will destroy the world on the day of judgment. Its former leader, Elijah Muhammad, believed that the biblical book of Ezekiel describes a "mother plane" or "wheel." The current leader, Louis Farrakhan, describes it like this:

> The Honorable Elijah Muhammad told us of a giant "Mother plane" that is made like the universe, spheres within spheres. White people call them unidentified flying objects (UFOs). Ezekiel,

in the Old Testament, saw a wheel that looked like a cloud by day but a pillar of fire by night. The Hon. Elijah Muhammad said that the wheel was built on the island of Nippon, which is now called Japan, by some of the original scientists. It took 15 billion dollars in gold at that time to build it. It is made of the toughest steel. America does not yet know the composition of the steel used to make an instrument like it. It is a circular plane, and the Bible says that it never makes turns. Because of its circular nature, it can stop and travel in all directions at speeds of thousands of miles per hour. He said there are 1,500 small wheels in this mother wheel, which is half a mile by a half a mile. This Mother Wheel is like a small human-built planet. Each one of these small planes carry three bombs."

It is thought by my Spirit Guides that the Hon. Elijah Muhammad did indeed get his information from the aliens aboard such a space craft during an abduction. Therefore, much of his information does not ring true, but is a type of propaganda that is a repeated theme of alien abductions.[11]

The International Raelian Movement

Our next group is that of Raelism. Known as The International Raelian Movement, Raelism has been described as one of, if not the largest, UFO religion in the world. Raelians believe extraterrestrials called "Elohim" created life on Earth by genetic engineering, and that a combination of mind transfer and cloning can ultimately grant us eternal life. They further believe that religious leaders, teachers, and prophets have been sent to us from the Elohim to teach humanity. These include Jesus, Buddha, and Muhammad. They believe also that the Elohim are planning a future visit, at which time they will complete their revelation and education of mankind. Raelism is represented now in fifty countries on five continents. In 1997, they announced that they would soon be able to clone people and whoever would like to clone themselves could do so for a fee of $200,000. This announcement made headlines at that time. The organization consists of six levels of responsibility, with the founder, Rael, at the top (sixth) level. On December 13th, 1973, Rael, then known as Claude Vorilhon, set up the Raelian movement after he was contacted by an alien visitor from another planet. The visitor, called an Elohim, was four feet in height, with long black hair, almond-shaped eyes, olive skin, and peace and harmony could be felt from him, as well as humor. He was told to establish an embassy for his people to welcome them to Earth. Allegedly, the alien told him that:

> We were the ones that made all life on Earth; you mistook us for gods; we were the origin of your main religions. Now that you are mature enough to understand this, we would like to enter official contact through an embassy.

In the days following his visitation, Rael, as he was named by the alien (which means "insignificant one" in Bru-Hoi language), "received commentaries on the most significant parts of the Bible." According to a book published by Rael called *Messages Given To Me by the Extraterrestrials*, he had another visitation in which they also gave him a ride in their space craft, all the way to their planet, called Elohim. He established the Raelian movement and is apparently working toward establishing an embassy to spread the Alien's message, and awaits their return.[12]

According to my Spirit Guides, there was a mining colony called Elohim, an odd choice for the name, and perhaps one that was chosen to insult Angeldom and Father at that time. This colony, too, is no longer in use. You see, Elohim is a term for a young Angel. Here is the Hierarchy of Angels:

1. Cherubim
   The children, with non functioning little wings.

2. Elohim
   Young adults, beginning their work. At 16 years, they learn how to fly and are given adult wings.

3. Seraphim
   Adults who have taken their final vows of poverty, chastity, and obedience.

4. Archangelorum
   The highest level. They can work in the private sector and still be given this rank. There are 46+ Arch Angels at this time.

Notice, also, that these alien visitors often wrap lies within a veneer of truth—the propaganda I spoke of earlier. Certainly, Heaven has sent us our prophets, teachers, and saints. The four-foot-high aliens with tan skin and almond eyes were most likely of Bru-Hoi or Bru-Hyashi extraction. I am told that they sometimes have blue eyes with the pupil visible, not always the very dark eyes, such as the "Roswell aliens."

Scientology

This now brings us to the UFO faith of Scientology. Scientology was founded by L. Ron Hubbard in the early 1950s. Mr. Hubbard published a number of books, and lectures which describe what he called a "Space Opera." Scientology uses Mr. Hubbard's theory of "lay psychotherapy" (Dianetics) as the basis of his religious philosophy. According to *The Oxford Dictionary of World Religions, 1997*, "Dianetics" deals with the "reactive mind," or subconscious. Scientology is concerned with the Thetan, or everlasting spirit. Mr. Hubbard believed that we are burdened by feelings of guilt accumulated over the course of many lifetimes. Through "auditing" or a form of lay counseling, our spirit is freed from this, so it can continue to grow. The movement has been accused of being aggressive, and on occasion, unlawful methods in its ways of recruitment and its methods of defense against critics, so that its short history has been surrounded by controversy.

While it is true that we are aliens on this planet, the idea that we were frozen and brought to Earth 75 million years ago by a ruler named Xenu is not true, according to my Spirit Guides. Mr. Hubbard also said that we have lived in many lifetimes, including lifetimes in ancient, advanced societies as "Helatrobus" and "Marcabians." Traumatic memories from these past lives are thought to be the reason for many present-day physical and mental ailments.[13] According to my Spirit Guides, neither Helatrobus or Marcabia has ever existed, at least as far as they are aware. Our universe is a very large place and if they existed, it was a very long time ago.

However, Mr. Hubbard does bring up a good point: even though our past lives have not been spent on Helatrobus, reincarnation does exist. It is true that we have almost certainly had past lives that have left a scar upon our subconscious. I can give myself as one example of this! I am afraid of water. I wanted to learn how to swim, but when I took a class, I began having memories of past lives come up and I had reoccurring dreams of a number of different scenarios in which I drowned. I learned the technique of swimming, but as yet, I have not overcome the powerful fear that would most likely cause me to panic and drown.

Once able to talk with my Spirit Guides on this subject, they told me that those memories that surfaced were indeed fragments of memories of my own death. In one, I am a Violinist (second violin) aboard the Titanic. I am an Irishman by the name of George Krims. We were ordered to stay and give the lifeboats to the women and children. We played on the deck, trying to keep down the panic. I recall the Captain walking slowly to the bow, and simply standing there. The deck pitched and then became almost vertical and I clawed at it, trying to hang on literally by my fingernails as first my violin and then I slid into the liquid blackness below.

The other fragment was of me as a child. I am walking down a wood-paneled hallway, with pictures on the walls on both sides. I am heading toward a Headmaster's office and I am filled with dread. As I approach, I see a figure in the doorway. He steps back one step, and then he turns his head toward me, and gives me an evil grin. He is an SS officer, who has found out that I am being hidden there in a Christian boarding school. I am Jewish and my parents somehow made this arrangement before they were taken away. I panic and run full tilt, to the opposite end of the hallway where there is an exit door—a fire escape on the outside of the building. I am running so fast that I miss the turn to go down the steps. Instead, I fly out over the rail into a small pond that was fairly close to the building. I cannot swim so I flounder, trying to survive. The SS Officer gets to me ahead of the Head Master, and I grab hold of his black leather boot, just the toe of it, as my hands are small, wet, and slippery. He takes the toe of his boot, places it on my forehead, and pushes me back under the water until I drown. I recall seeing the older couple who owned the school, as they ran out to help me. My name was Helga Reinhold and I was of Austrian descent. However, the school was in Germany, I am told by my Spirit Guides. Once I understood all of this, the dreams stopped reoccurring, but the fear of water remains.

I personally think that most of us do have scars created by such experiences and that often they surface as mine did when I tried to learn to swim. This does not mean that I am in agreement with Mr. Hubbard, however. According to Mr. Hubbard, when we Thetans (human souls) die, we go to a "landing station" on the planet Venus, where we are then implanted and programmed to "forget" our past lives, thus causing amnesia. The Venusians then "capsule each soul" and sends them back to Earth to be dumped into the ocean off the coast of California, whereupon we souls have to search for another body to inhabit.[13a] There are not enough words to express how very much I disagree with that scenario!

The Unarius Academy

The Unarius Academy of Science was founded by Ernest L. Norman and his wife, Ruth, in 1954. This church is headquartered in El Cajon, California. They believe that through the use of 4th-dimensional physics, they can communicate with alien beings that exist on a higher frequency plane. Unarians believe in past lives and hold that the solar system was at one time inhabited by "ancient interplanetary civilizations." Now, we on Earth are in the 3rd dimension, our Guardians and the out-of-body souls around us on this planet are in the 4th dimension. Parutia (Heaven), Father, and our people are located in the 5th dimension. I doubt that the laws of physics are applied any differently in the 4th dimension than they are in our third. However, I am not a physicist. Our overall frequencies show up in our auras. I am told that back home, we have people whose auras are at different frequencies such as green, blue, yellow, indigo, etc., just as we have on our world in this dimension.[14] However, it is possible that Mr. and Mrs. Norman may have been told that they were being contacted by "4th dimensional physicists." Also, reincarnation is a fact, or it is seen that way on Parutia, (Heaven). They most likely were talking to someone from another planet in the 5th dimension (thus, aliens) and it is true that our solar system was once inhabited by two other groups of people, long before Father sent us to earth to colonize it.

The Universe People

The Universe People is a Czech movement started by Ivo A. Benda in 1997. The group has also been known as "Cosmic People of Light Powers." Their belief system is derived from the communications Mr. Benda has had with various extraterrestrial groups that he and other "Contacters" have had since October of 1997. These communications took place, at first, by telepathy, and then by direct contact. Benda maintains that these civilizations operate a fleet of spaceships led by Ashtar Sheran. I am advised by my Spirit Guides that this is the name of a commander of one of the "Regatta Morte" or death ships that are responsible for carrying many souls to work within mining colonies! Ashtar, supposedly, told Mr. Benda that this fleet orbits Earth, closely monitoring us, helping the good and waiting to transport the followers into another dimension.[15] Other Universe People teachings are that Jesus was a "fine-vibrations" being, and that "forces of evil are supposed to plan compulsory chipping of the populace (here on Earth). Commander Ashtar Sheran and his people resided in the same constellation that Parutians (we) do, back home. However, when I was writing this book, his superiors heard of the lies told to the Terrans (Earth people). It is an unhappy fact that what I write or say is often monitored. The lies told by Commander Ashtar Sheran to our people proved to be a political embarrassment and he became Private Sheran, until war destroyed his world, recently.

Ashtar Sheran most likely told Mr. Benda that forces of evil planned to chip away at our world populace, when in fact, he and others from his planet were the very ones ordered to do this! According to my Spirit Guides, it is a fact that he and his people are servants of The Darkness, not Father.

Among other UFO religions and visitations of note, Mr. Benjamin Crème, who is a Theosophical teacher, says that the Messiah figure called Maitreya (May-Tray-Ah), will soon declare himself publicly and is said to be in telepathic contact with "the space brothers" in their flying saucers.[15a] The truth, according to my Spirit Guides, is that Commander Maitreya most likely continued to serve the same government as Commander Ashtar Sheran. Neither one belongs to Parutia (Heaven). Mr. Crème believes that "Nordic Aliens" from Venus pilot flying saucers from a civilization on Venus that exists there on the etheric plane and is very ancient. He believes that they have motherships that are four miles long. It is also believed that the "governing deity of Earth," Sanat Kumara (who is believed to live in a city called Shamballa, located above the Gobi desert, on the etheric plane of Earth), is himself, a "Nordic Alien" who came to Earth from Venus 18,500,000 years ago. According to my Spirit Guides, First Officer Sanat Kumara was commissioned by his own government and served aboard the same vessel as Commander Ashtar Sheran. I am also advised that First Officer Sunat Kumara was by no means Nordic in appearance, but "short, dark, and some what hairy."

The Ascended Master Teachings

Another group of Theosophic-based religions is called "The Ascended Master Teachings," specifically using those teachings by Joshua David Stone. In 1993, Stone began to refer to Ashtar as an Ascended Master. He continued including Ashtar on his list of Ascended Masters that he received information from, when speaking at his Wesak Festival Mount Shasta gatherings that have been held since 1996. Stone also taught that the Master Jesus, under his "galactic name Sananda" sometimes rides with Commander Ashtar in his flying saucer fleet. Now, If I have not already said this, allow me to be very clear: Sananda is the soul who was once known as Jesus or Christ in that lifetime here on Earth. He now resides on Parutia, or Heaven, where he works closely with Father! Sananda serves Father and Heaven, not the group of people that Commander Ashtar served. It is very obvious that the Commander Ashtar Sheran wanted this bit of misinformation to find its way back to Father and to Sananda as an insult, or simply to aggravate. "Master Jesus," back home on Parutia, would mean "Little Jesus" or "Young Jesus," so the intent to have a joke at Sananda's expense is clear.[15b]

Tempelhofgesellschaft and Marcionism

Lastly, a group in Vienna, Austria, called Tempelhofgesellschaft was founded in the early 1990s and is a neo-Nazi Gnostic Sect. It teaches a form of "Marcionism." They claim that the Aryan race originally came to Atlantis from the star Aldebaran, and that this information was gleaned from "ancient Sumerian manuscripts." They believe that the Aryan race is of extraterrestrial origin and has a divine mission to dominate all of the other races. They believe that a huge fleet of space ships are on the way to Earth from Aldebaran, and that they in turn will join forces with the Nazi Flying Saucers from Antarctica to establish their supremacy.[16] This is a good example, once again, of a twisted truth being couched in untruths. First of all, Atlantis was our first attempt to colonize Earth. I spoke of this in our first chapter. We do not recognize that there is any imperative to dominate others, ever. This is not a part of Father's teachings, and it never will be. Secondly, Aldebaran was yet another illegal mining colony, which has been gone now for a very long time. There was a group of people who were called Aryans. These were the people that colonized the area now known as India. It is known that another, older group of people were already in that area, but little is known about them or where they came from. The Aryans fought them and then subjugated them, in order to claim the area around the Indus River valley. According to my Spirit Guides, although it is not known for a fact, it is thought that the Aryans became the victors and so the ruling class and those conquered became the "untouchables" of Indian society. The Aryans were not in any way Nordic, or blonde-haired or blue-eyed. They were of Draconian extraction, and would have olive skin and dark hair and eyes.

Changing the subject a bit, a local site that deserves our attention is that of the "Judaculla Rock." It is located in Sylva, North Carolina, in the southwestern part of the state. It is thought that the rock is 2,000 to 3,000 years old. This rock is covered with some type of petroglyphs that have never been translated, at least not at the writing of this book. The Cherokee Indians see this rock as ancient and according to their legend, the markings were created by a giant named "Judaculla." He was considered to be a great Lord of the Hunt, who could leap from mountain to mountain and could also control the weather. It is thought that this rock once saved him from a fall, and that the hand print with seven fingers that can be seen upon the rock is his.

When I first heard about the Judaculla Rock several years ago, I was intrigued. There is a line across the rock that might denote air and land or water and land. The seven-fingered hand print might actually be denoting sea life such as an octopus. In fact, a smaller one beside it has three legs or fingers and seems to be swimming beside the larger one, perhaps an octopus and her young. According to my Spirit Guides, there are some symbols recognizable as early Parutian nomenclature, which suggests that space travelers who perhaps came to settle the area, might have put some marks there on this rock. It could have been a tribute or perhaps it was there to show others the way to a village. I am told by my Spirit Guides that the marks that they recognized were directional. We may never know the secrets of this rock, or why more than one group carved upon it. According to Robert McGhee of the web site called shadowbox.brinkster.net/judaculla.

html, many college students from Western Carolina University have held late night, secret initiations and these ceremonies have provoked a paranormal response. Strange noises at or around the stone, as well as illuminations around the rock itself have been noted. There also have been reports of UFOs above this clearing, according to Mr. McGhee.[17] The stone is located at the base of a mountain and a large vein of copper runs under this site. Such a scenario may create electrical anomalies that are detectable with equipment such as a K-2 (electromagnetic) meter.

I haven't found evidence as yet to suggest that anyone has attempted to measure such readings.

The *Archeo News* at Stonepages.com/news/ Archives, January 2004, advises that the name was taken from the Cherokee name for the slant-eyed giant "Tsulkalu." It was difficult to pronounce and the Europeans changed it to Judaculla, pronounced "Ju-da-coo-lah." Scott Ashcraft, staff archaeologist for the U.S. Forestry Service, says that the rock is made of soap stone, and it sits on a deposit of soap stone, not copper. It is my belief, if memory serves me, that soap stone, as well as metal ores, can create the right environment for electromagnetic anomalies and paranormal activity. Perhaps this stone and others like it that have been found along the North Carolina and Tennessee border have given directions to space ships as well as those who traveled on foot to some unknown village. Native Americans are thought to be partly Draconian and partly Asian (*Chin Wah-zei*) with the possibility of another lesser known group in their heritage as well. It is possible that in the early days of such colonies, their colleagues visited from their native worlds and perhaps traded with them, just as they undoubtedly did with the Nazcas and other tribes. Could it be that the Val Gorin or the Zan-Besii had a colony in the Carolinas at one time? The Cherokee recognized an area called "Inzignanin," which indicated that the "Fish People" lived there. According to my Shamanic Spirit Guide, no one returned from visiting this place, and it was thought that they had been invited to join the Fish People. Sadly, we will never know for sure.

The Nazca Lines Whale, aerial view. *Courtesy trg31, www.bigstockphoto.com.*

Mayan Carving. Bru-Hyashi?

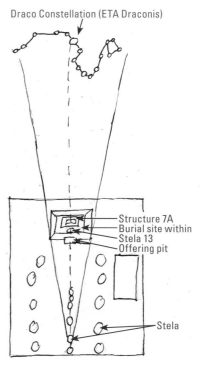

Draco Constellation (ETA Draconis)

Structure 7A
Burial site within
Stela 13
Offering pit

Stela

Structure 7 of Takalik Abaj

Stone Crocodile.
Takalik Abaj.

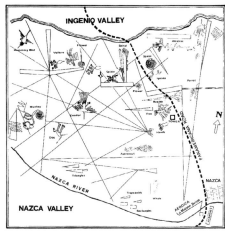

Map of Nazca Lines.

Sketch of ruins at Takalik Abaj.

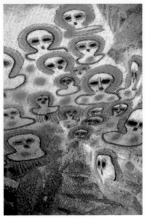

Cave art suggests that the
people of Val Carmonica, Italy,
knew the Bru-Hyashi.

Astronauts? Cave painting from
Val Carmonica.

Sandoolah

I took a picture of a stray cat in my backyard and found the
commander in the snapshot. I was told that he knew me from my
previous abduction.

Moa, Easter Island

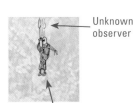

Unknown
observer

Comm. Ashtar Sheran

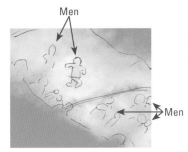

Men

Men

Tunnel between shuttles or ship to shuttle. These are called
"Skywalks." The generic name is "Temporary Dissolving
Enscarpment," I am told.

CHAPTER FOUR

They Do Not Come in Peace

For quite some time now, there have been reports of cattle, goats, horses, and other animals being found mutilated, many with surgical precision. Most have officially been categorized as random acts of a disturbed person or persons unknown. Others have been extensively investigated and ruled animal attacks or as probable natural death, with bacterial activity rupturing the abdomens. Many have been found with no footprints around the remains and frequently without blood, as if they were completely drained. There have been cases in which these poor animals have been found impaled in the tops of trees, or autopsies have shown extensive injury such as multiple fractures compatible with having been dropped from a great height.

You have seen in the preceding photos, a deer draped around a power line. It is nearly impossible to imagine that this was done by one person or even a group. That animal would weigh several hundred pounds, and the person or persons who did this would be at risk of being electrocuted. The logical assumption, then, would be that the animal was dropped from a helicopter or plane. Possibly, but most likely it was a shuttle craft or small craft used in cases of alien abductions. Such crafts emit almost no noise and could be used to accomplish this faster and more efficiently than anything we have currently on Earth. Helicopters would make noise that would cause other animals, especially on a farm or ranch, to cry out and alert the owners that something was wrong. This, of course, would depend on the size of the farm, and if there were neighbors close to the area in question.

Varied individuals have said that the deer was hit by a train and thrown to this position. I haven't found anything to prove what actually happened to this poor deer, but I do find it very hard to believe that a train did this. The animal is very high and precariously balanced there. Additionally, it has no hooves, part of it's legs are gone, and you can see Doobisee or Sandoolahs around it. According to my Spirit Guides, "We are aware of the situation and we are currently doing everything we can to insure that this does not continue, but it has not been an easy matter to resolve. Even our Father must adhere to the letter of the law." They have also told me that the deer was in fact dropped onto the powerline by shuttle, which would make very little noise when in flight.

A gentleman by the name of Charles Fort collected information concerning cattle mutilations in the late 19th and early 20th centuries in England.[18] However, such reports began to surface in the United States in the early 1960s. At that time, most of these reports seemed to center around farms in Pennsylvania and Kansas.

In 1967, a Colorado newspaper published a story about a horse named Lady, who was found mutilated. This story was picked up and published nationwide and was the first to include speculation that aliens or extraterrestrials might be involved. The incident occurred near Alamosa,Colorado, in 1967. It was September 7th, and the owner, Agnes King, and her son noted that Lady had not returned from the pasture that evening. On Sept. 9th, Lady was found mutilated. Her head and neck were denuded and the bones white and clean. There was no blood at the scene, and the incisions seemed precise. According to Mrs. King's son, Harry, there was a strong medicinal scent in the air. On the 10th, Mrs. King returned to the site with Mr. and Mrs. Berle Lewis, who were Mrs. King's brother and sister-in-law. They found a lump of horse flesh and skin that oozed a greenish fluid. When touched, this fluid burned her hand. They also reported the presence of fifteen "tapering exhaust marks" punched into the ground over approximately 5,000 yards. The medicinal odor was still present. An investigation was undertaken by the U.S. Forest Service and a Ranger by the name of Duane Martin. Ranger Martin used a Geiger counter to check the area and found increased radiation over an area the size of two city blocks.[19]

Mrs. Lewis tried to no avail to interest other authorities in carrying out a more extensive investigation. She occasionally wrote for the *Pueblo Chieftain*, and write she did! Her article was picked up by the Associated Press on October 5, 1967. In the wake of Lady's death, other cases began to emerge. That same day, interestingly enough, an account was published by a Superior Court Judge Charles E. Bennett of Denver, Colorado. He claimed that he and his wife saw "three reddish orange rings in the sky. They maintained a triangular formation, moved at high speed and made a humming sound." A UFO Research group, the National Investigations Committee On Aerial Phenomena (NICAP), speculated that UFOs were involved. A short time after this, an anonymous pathologist from Denver published an account of the necropsy. Lady's brain and abdominal organs were removed and her spinal cord was also missing.[20] A pathologist by the name of Dr. Robert O. Adams (Head of Colorado State University Veterinary and Biomedical Science School) was called in to examine the remains. He concluded that there were no "unearthly causes, at least not to his mind." He further stated that the saddle pony had an severe infection in her hind quarters and he speculated that someone probably had come across the dying horse and slit its throat to end its suffering! Dr. Adams then said that the rest of the damage was done by natural predators. Mrs. Lewis was not in agreement with Dr. Adams, and said that his findings did not account for the lack of blood at the scene or the medicinal odor which was present as well. Robert Low, coordinator for the Condon Committee at the University of Colorado, who had brought Dr. Adams into the case, claimed that they had found the anonymous Doctor who published the necropsy report. He was said not to be a pathologist at all, but a hematologist by the name of Dr. John H. Altshuler.[21] I do not have any legal proof of what I am about to say; however, according to my Spirit Guides, Dr. John Altshuler was paid to take the responsibility for the necropsy report that was published. They (my Spirit Guides) are familiar with the case and how it affected those involved. They wish me to relate to all of you that the original report of that anonymous pathologist was the accurate one. By 1970, cattle mutilations had been reported in fifteen states, including Montana, South Dakota, New Mexico, and Texas.[22] Democratic Senator Floyd K. Haskell asked the FBI for their help in investigating these cases due to public concern. At that time, Senator Haskell had identified 130 cases of cattle mutilations in Colorado alone.[23]

Perhaps the most disturbing was an account which involved a human being. There is documented photographic evidence of a mutilation of a man, whose name has been withheld by the request of his family. The incident took place outside of Sao Paulo, Brazil, in 1994 or 1988—various websites are offering the police photos of this man's remains, but there are inconsistencies in the stories told. I have no doubt whatsoever that this murder occurred, and the exact date is not important to the reporting of this incident in this case. His body was found near Guaraperanga Reservoir. There was no sign of a struggle or of bondage being used. There were no signs of decay or animal predation, no odor, nor bleeding. His left eye was removed, his left eyelid was removed, his ear was removed, his lips excised, and the side of his left jaw was taken. The jaw bone was also removed. These were done with a surgical precision that suggested laser surgical tools. His tongue was removed, and the mouth cavity emptied. In short, his mutilation wounds were very typical of the cattle mutilations that we have been speaking of. The medical examiners concluded that none of the wounds were due to bullets, and **the procedure more than likely occurred while the victim was still alive and the associated pain resulted in cardiac arrest and subsequent death.**[24]

There are defining characteristics that make the death of an animal more likely to be a true cattle or animal mutilation, rather than a death of natural causes. In most cases, the body has been drained of blood. Often, there is no sign of blood around or on the outside of the body. A typical case would involve many or all of the following:

1. Removal of eyes, udders, and sexual organs of cows very cleanly with surgical precision

2. The removal of the anus to a depth of around twelve inches, similar in appearance to surgical coning.

3. The removal of the lips, and/or tongue, deeply cut out from the throat.

4. The removal of one ear.

5. The removal of major organs, such as heart or liver, with no exit or entry marks. Often, if the heart is missing, there is no excision wound and the pericardium is still intact with the heart missing.

6. The stripping of hide and flesh from the jaw and the area directly beneath the ear to the bone.

7. The removal of soft organs from the lower body.

8. The presence of incisions and cuts across the body that appear to have been made by a surgical instrument.

9. Unexplained damage to remaining organs without any sign of damage to the surrounding area.

10. A lack of predation signs (including teeth marks, tearing of the skin or flesh, and a lack of animal foot prints) on or around the carcass.

11. In many cases, a draining of most of the blood from the animal. The blood that remains shows color changes and may not coagulate for days.

12. The animal will appear dumped or dropped in a secluded area, with no animal, human, or vehicle tracks leading to or from the site. Some have been found draped over fences or treetops as if dropped from over head.

13. The ground under the animal appears depressed, as if the animal was dropped on the site from a great height, leaving an impact crater.

14. The animal's bones are found to be fractured with injuries consistent with being dropped.

15. Strange marks or holes in the ground around the carcass.

16. Other cattle avoid the carcass and the area where it is found.

17. Eyewitness reports of aerial objects or UFOs seen in the vicinity at the time of the animal going missing.[25]

It is interesting to note that higher or lower amounts of vitamins and minerals have been found in tissue samples of these animals, but not in all. In one case, in 1978 in New Mexico, a bull belonging to a Mr. Gomez of Dulce was found mutilated. The remains exhibited many of the signs listed here, including the removal of the rectum and sex organs. According to Gabriel L. Veldez of the New Mexico Police, both the heart and liver were white and mushy and both had the consistency of peanut butter. Liver samples were completely free of copper, but contained four times the normal amount of zinc, potassium, and phosphorus. Blood samples revealed that the bull's blood was light pink, and did not clot for several days. The animal's hide was found to be too brittle for a fresh kill and the flesh beneath was discolored. During the early stages of the investigation, it was postulated that a short burst of radiation might have been used to kill the animal, and that this had caused the red blood cells to burst. However, this idea was dropped when it was revealed that the presence of an anti-coagulant had been found in other cases of cattle mutilation in that area.[26]

In May of 1979, the Federal authorities launched an investigation of these cattle mutilations. The study cost $44,170, which was paid by a grant through the Law Enforcement Assistance Administration. This project was headed by FBI Agent Kenneth Rommel. Rommel's final report of 297 pages concluded that these mutilation cases were predominately caused by natural animal predation, but he did concede that there were some findings that could not be accounted for by any conventional thought. The FBI also could not find any information that would identify the individuals responsible for these acts.

Just before the FBI investigation, there was a State level investigation led by law enforcement officials in New Mexico. Their findings showed evidence that some cattle had been given tranquilizers and anti-coagulants prior to the mutilations. This investigation was headed by Officer Gabriel L. Veldez of the New Mexico Police and assisted by Cattle Inspector Jim Dyad and Officer Howard Johnston of the New Mexico Department of Game and Fishery.

It is my impression that many explanations have been brought forward in an attempt to find a rational reason and explanation for these bizarre animal killings. In essence, they can be categorized into three categories:

1. Predators
2. Parasites
3. Scavengers

The work of carrion beetles, carrion birds, such as vultures and buzzards, and blowflies have been sited as a possible cause in the cases. Also, such things as postmortem bloat, which causes the body to swell and eventually rupture and tear the skin; and solar desiccation, which can degrade and evaporate fluids and blood components, reducing the volume of blood have also been noted.

However, there are aspects of these mutilations which cannot be explained away by natural predation. In fact, it has been noted that in any number of cases, other animals would not go near the corpses. The evidence that some had been dropped from a great height, even causing some of the bodies to be impaled in tree tops or on top of power lines is another aspect. The smell of chemicals or that caustic green ooze found in the case of Lady, the horse, as well as the medicinal odor cannot be easily explained. The fact that anti-coagulants and tranquilizers have been isolated from tissue samples is still another factor.[27] In many cases, the incisions were too precise to be caused by postmortem bloat. What could cause the heart and liver to be the consistency of peanut butter, and the hide to be brittle, as if the corpse were much older? It is impossible to believe that poor health could explain such cases.

In fact, according to one cattle mutilations article, many ranchers have reported that these cattle were amongst the strongest and healthiest in their herd. According to the same source, there are several theories that can be derived from the mutilation of animals:

- The mutilation by predatory animals (but how can we dismiss the blood thinners and other anomalies?)

- That of deviant human behavior. There are, after all, people who derive sexual pleasure from the mutilation and killing of animals. Sociopaths who sometimes cross over to human mutilations and killing after practice with animals. I cite the sad case of Mr. Jeffrey Dahmer as one example.[28]

- The ceremonies and rituals of various cults have also been suspect where cattle/animal mutilation has occurred. Satanism, Witchcraft, Santeria, and Vodun (Voodoo) have all fallen suspect during the investigation of such crimes.

Religious Implications

Witchcraft, or as it is known in the United States, Wicca, is considered to be one of the very oldest of religions. Wicca is a contemporary pagan religion that has its roots in shamanism. It is also a nature spirit religion that predates Christianity. They worship our creator/supreme God as a god/goddess duality. They also practice magic rituals that are "white" or positive and good, but can also practice rituals that are "black" or negative and harmful as well.

I am told that our Father does not object to the doctrine or basic teachings of Wicca—respecting nature and seeing Father as a god/goddess duality. However, he does not like the practice of magic spells, regardless of whether or not they are good or bad in their intent. Why? Because we are not strong enough, here on Earth, to bring about something by the use of magic. Recall, if you will, that we are only a small part of our higher selves, or an aspect. Now, Father will not help those of us who practice magic. Our Spirit Guides in Heaven and our Guardians here with us on Earth will not, either. Therefore, if we cast a spell and it really happens, who is helping us? The Demons or Jinn. They will help us with good works and make us feel very powerful and connected. They will then work to gradually push us over to the bad or dark spells. Magic, then, gives the evil ones a window to your soul.

Vodun, sometimes called "**Voodoo**," is a religion which originated with the West African Yoruba people in the 18th and 19th century in the country of Dahomey, Togo, Benin, and Nigeria, all on land that was a part of Dahomey at that time. Vodun is an ancestral and nature religion. Its name is derived from the African word for "Spirit." It has taken root in Haiti, and most of the adult population now practices Vodun.[29]

Currently, many major cities in the United States of America have groups of worshipers of Vodun. When slaves were abducted in Africa and taken to the U.S.A., they were often baptized into the Roman Catholic Church. However, the teachings of Christianity were not given to them, and they followed their own religion. They may have attended Mass regularly, but they practiced their own faith in secret.

Because Vodun is an ancestral nature religion, the practitioners feel a strong connection with their deities. They believe that lessons can be learned equally from all paths to the truth. Therefore, they honor their ancestors, even the ones who were perhaps infamous or notorious. Each Vodun group worships a slightly different pantheon of spirits called Loa.[30] This word means "mystery" in the Yoruba language. They believe in a chief God Olorun, a lesser God Obatala, and hundreds of minor Gods. The comparison between Christianity and Vodun can give one pause. These are their "points of similarity":

1. Both believe in a supreme being.

2. The Loa resemble Catholic Saints, in that they were once people who led exceptional lives and are usually given a single responsibility or special attribute.

3. Both believe in an afterlife.

4. Both have as a centerpiece of some of their ceremonies, a ritual sacrifice and consumption of flesh and blood. This would mirror the Holy Eucharist, the belief that the body and blood of Christ are present in the communion bread.

5. Both believe in the existence of invisible spirits and demons.

6. Followers of Vodun believe that each person has a "Met Tet" or "master of the head," which might correspond to a Christian's Patron Saint.[31]

Followers of Vodun believe that we all have a soul that has two parts: a "gros bon ange" or "Big Good Angel," and a "ti bon ange" or "Small Good Angel." The small one leaves the body during sleep and may be captured by evil sorcery during that vulnerable time.

Contact with the Loa is made by sacrifice of animals and by gifts. They provide health, protection from evil spirits, and good fortune, in exchange for the gifts of food. Rituals are held during times of celebration of good fortune, lucky events, and to escape from bad fortune as well as birth, marriage, healing and death.[32] I have heard it said that, in Christianity, one worships his God in Heaven, but in Vodun, one worships his Gods who are everywhere, both in and around him.

Vodun Priests may be male or female. A Vodun Temple is called a **hounfour** or **humfort**. At the center is a pole, which is where the gods communicate with the believers. There will be an altar, which includes candles, picture of Catholic Saints and items that are symbolic of or pleasing to the Loas. There is usually a feast before the ceremony, and a pattern of flour on the floor, called a **Veve** that is unique to the Loa. Each Loa has his own pattern or identifying symbol, or Veve. There is chanting and the shaking of a rattle and drumming, with instruments that have been blessed. They dance with increasing intensity, until some become possessed by a Loa. They may then act as the Loa, and are given respect. Then there is an animal sacrifice. This may be a goat, sheep, chicken, or dog. They

are usually killed humanely and the blood is collected in a vessel. The possessed dancers may drink some of the blood. Having satisfied the hunger of the Loa, the animal is usually cooked and eaten. Animal sacrifice consecrates the meat for the followers who eat it, as well as the followers of Vodun, their gods, and ancestors. The priests and priestesses of Vodun are to practice "white or good" magic. These are called Houngans or Mambos. The practitioners of "black magic" or harmful spells are called "Caplatas," or "Bokors." It is rare for a practitioner of white magic to participate in spells that are harmful, but there may be a few that alternate between the two.

When one thinks of Vodun, images of such horror movie classics such as depicting zombies come to mind. This is not fiction to practitioners of Vodun. My Spirit Guides inform me that this practice is considered very dark and evil and would be undertaken by a Bokor. They tell me that they have never known such a spell to work, but tales and stories are still found within Vodun. A zombie is created by a web of magic, herbs, and probably very strong drugs. These drugs would be given to create the illusion of death. The person would be buried, then dug up. At this time, the person would be the property or at the mercy of the sorcerer who poisoned him.

When I think of zombies, I recall a horror movie based upon a book called *The Serpent and the Rainbow* and a movie of the same name. It tells of a scientist who travels to Haiti to procure a sample of a drug said to be used to create zombies. It ends up being a complicated recipe that includes the poison from poisonous frogs and other ingredients. His employer wanted to see if it could be refined as another type of anesthetic, because it sounded as if it worked in a similar way to the drug Curare, commonly used to relax internal organs and muscles during major surgery. In the film, it is found that the drug rendered the person unable to move or speak, but they were aware, they were not unconscious. I do not know how much of the movie is true, but it is based on a true scientist and his personal account of his search for this substance.

Could Vodun ritual account for all of the animal mutilations in this country? In my personal opinion, no. Vodun, as we have learned, is a nature spirit and ancestral religion. They believe in the humane killing of animals that are sacrificed. They also cook and eat the animals that they kill. Vodun believers believe in honoring their dead, they believe that they are guided by direct intervention of the spirits who come to them during their rituals, to offer spiritual guidance and blessings. The kind of cruel, hideous mutilations that have been found in Colorado and elsewhere have been anything but respectful of life or spiritual. It is my own belief that practitioners of Vodun would see this as something they might ultimately be punished for by the Loas they worship.[33]

Santeria is another religion that has been suspected of performing animal mutilations. According to *The Oxford Dictionary of World Religions*, Santeria (*Cuban, The Way of The Saints*), this is a complex of religious cults in the Afro-Cuban population, combining Yoruba African and Spanish Catholic traditions, especially concerning the saints (santos) who are identified with the spirits (Orishas) of the Yoruba Pantheon. Each worshipper may have a personal patron saint and belong to a cult group or congregation under a priest, with a great variety among the groups. Where Santeria closely follows Roman Catholic rites, it is hard to distinguish from Catholicism; other forms emphasize trance possession (also seen in Vodun) by the spirits or Orishas. Worship features prayers and songs in Yoruba, drumming, which may speak for the spirits, and sacred stones of power, associated with the spirits, kept under the altar, baptized, and fed annually with herbs and blood.[34] These cults endeavour to control and use the spirits for practical benefits, but lack any ethical requirements; their main growth since the Castro revolution has been among Cuban exiles, especially in the United States.

Santeria, also known as **Lukumi**, was brought to the Caribbean via the slave trade, and came to America during the Cuban exodus of the 1960s. There are, as of 2007, over 3 to 4 million practitioners of Santeria in the United States. One source tells of a Santeria priest who filed a federal discrimination lawsuit against the city of Euless, Texas. The suit was to decide if those practicing Santeria would be allowed to sacrifice animals during their rituals within the city limits of the town.[35] Santeria, as with other less than main stream faiths, has largely remained underground, with services and rituals being practiced in the homes of the priests or members. Euless has a law which prohibits the killing of animals within the city limits, thus the reason for the lawsuit.[36]

Jose Merced came to the U.S. from Puerto Rico in 1990. Apparently, complaints began when he became the only Santeria Oba (Father) in the area. Neighbors began complaining about noise, the smell and cry of animals, loud chanting, and parking issues. According to Mr. Merced, animal sacrifice is such an important part of Santeria that Santeria would cease to exist without it.[37] The Orisha spirits emanate from God and can only manifest through the energy of blood from the sacrificed animal. In this interview, he says that it is the sacrifice and blood that makes a priest a priest. That is to say, it is an integral part of their ordination rites. Mr. Merced likens their animal sacrifice to the Holy Eucharist in that if you remove the act of communion, of eating and drinking the body and blood of Jesus Christ, you would no longer have a Christian or Catholic Mass. The animals that are sacrificed are then cleaned and cooked in a stew and eaten in a feast.[38]

As with Vodun, Santeria has a dark side. Santeria seeks to work with and to possibly control the forces of good, to work within the light. The dark side of Santeria is called **Palo Mayombe**. I wish to emphasize that I do not recommend that anyone joins or even investigates a religious sect or cult, most especially one that pays homage to Satan, the demons, or to any deities that are of evil. I suspect that the practitioners of Palo Mayombe would tell me that they worship the same ones as Santeria, but are asking for different results. I have been told by our Father and my Spirit Guides repeatedly that Father does not care what faith we are here on this Earth as long as we show him a good life. However, the two directions that he does not like us to follow are Satanism and any religion that involves spell casting, good or bad. I can't stress this enough.

Now, this being said, let us talk about the "dark side of Santeria." According to my references, this type of Santeria originated in the African Congo and is considered to be the most feared and most powerful form of black magic. Those who practice this are called **Palero**. With the slave trade, it spread to Cuba and Puerto Rico in the 1500s. The influence of Palo Mayombe can be felt in Central America, Brazil, and Mexico. In Brazil, it is called **Quimbanda** and there it is said to be a mixture of African Congo and Latin American spirituality.[39] The difference between Santeria and Palo Mayombe is that Santeria does call upon the forces of good, or light, where as Palo Mayombe calls upon the forces of darkness or evil. Palo Mayombe has its own priesthood, and its own set of rules and regulations and most members of Santeria avoid being associated with practitioners of Palo Mayombe. These rules and regulations may vary according to the house or group that a person is initiated into. Once again, according to my reference, it is said that a Palero Priest can bring about the death of an individual within twenty-four hours, and that they can take a man of obscure origins and turn him into a powerful world figure in a short period of time.

I beg you to remember what I have said about magic spells and the fact that here on Earth we cannot make them work by ourselves. The Paleros are obviously and deliberately working with the demons in order to cast such spells successfully. They aren't making a spell work, evil is. The house of the dead, we are told, is where the Palero Spirits reside. We are also told that these spirits are so evil and strong that they cannot reside with the Santos of Santeria. A Palero, then may keep his spirits in a special spirit house, outside. This place may be a room, in case of an apartment, and the light must be very dim, with a candle burning in their honor at all times. I am told that Paleros work by referral and never advertise. It is also said to be a lifelong commitment and should never be dabbled in or trivialized.[40]

As with Santeria, the Paleros recognize the seven African Powers:

1. **Eleggua:** Saint Anthony of Padua, red and black
2. **Obatala:** Our Lady of Mercy, white
3. **Chango:** Saint Barbara, red and white
4. **Oggun:** Saint Peter, green and black
5. **Orunla:** Saint Francis of Assisi, green, yellow
6. **Yemaya:** Our Lady of Regla, white and blue
7. **Oshun:** Our Lady of La Curidad del Cobre, yellow, coral, and aquamarine
8. **Baba-Lu-Aye:** Saint Lazarus, Royal Purple
9. **Aquanyu-Sola:** Saint Christopher, red
10. **Oya:** Our Lady of Candlemas, all colors except black, she likes wine color the best.[41]

Although my research did not verify this, it is my belief that, as with Santeria and Vodun, the animals sacrificed are most likely killed humanely and eaten after the ceremony. Therefore, it is unlikely, but not impossible, that they would be responsible for the cattle mutilations. When dealing with evil, however, the main rule is often that there are no rules. The more evil, hateful, or disgraceful the crime or the rite, the more the evil ones will like it. Therefore, it is possible that in Palo Mayombe a sacrificed animal may be left to rot or to be found by its owner for maximum revulsion. Like Vodun and Santeria, it is also considered a type of ancestor worship.

Now we must address Witchcraft and Satanism as suspects. Witchcraft, or **Wicca**, as it is now widely known, is one of the oldest nature spirit and god/goddess religions. According to *The Oxford Dictionary of World Religions*:

> ...The belief that human affairs and features of the environment can be ordered, controlled, and changed by skilled practitioners

whose powers are usually believed to be innate. Witchcraft is closely associated with magic, but its techniques are derived from within or given by a supernatural agent, rather than learned...the belief that the agent was the devil led to ferocious persecution of witches in medieval Christian Europe...an antagonist reinforced by the fact that since the activity of witches frequently lies outside the boundaries of customary social behaviours, they are often feared.

It goes on to say

...this tradition is often known as Wicca or Wicce, from the old English root which means to shape or to bend, but it is embedded in a wider neo-paganism. According to StarHawk, a leader of the recovery of Wicca, followers of Wicca seek their inspiration in pre-Christian sources, European folk lore, and mythology. They consider themselves priests and priestesses of an ancient European Shamanistic nature religion that worships a goddess who is related to the ancient mother goddess in her three aspects of the maiden, mother, and crone. She protests against the caricature of witches as members of a kooky cult, and claims that Wicca has the depth, dignity, and seriousness of purpose of a true religion.[42]

Witchcraft, as defined in *The Complete Book of Oils and Brews* is:

the craft of the witch-magic, especially magic utilizing personal power in conjunction with the energies within stones, herbs, colors, and other natural objects, some followers of Wicca use this word to denote their religion, producing much confusion on the part of outsiders.[43]

Witchcraft and Wicca, then, is a neo-pagan religion that recognizes the souls and the innate energies in all of nature. Witchcraft can, however, seek to do good, or white magic, or it can also be used to harm, or black magic." Having read and perused four books on the subject, I can say that not one of them spoke about animal sacrifices. In a brief article found on line in *The Pagan Institute Report*:

Wiccans are said to occasionally practice "bloodletting" in certain rituals, although they deny practicing animal sacrifices or mutilation. According to this article, some female witches use their own blood in spells..."and offer a drop or two of their own blood" during a spell. "But the only blood a witch has the right to offer is her/his own.[44]

It is my personal belief that as a religion that respects and even deifies nature and that professes to work only for the common good, it is unlikely that Wicca could be implicated in the cattle mutilations in this country. There is a "harm none" clause that Wiccans must take when initiated into the craft. Laurie Cabot, founder of The Witches League for Public Awareness in Salem, Massachusetts, states that Witchcraft is based on three principles, the first of which is "Do what you will, and harm none."[45] However, it is not impossible for those who are practicing Black Magic. As I have stated before, I have been told by my Spirit Guides that one of the reasons that Father does not want us to practice any type of magic is that once we begin to feel powerful, it gradually becomes easier to sway us into practicing Black Magic, instead of spells used for the common good. Because the bad spells are being encouraged or fueled by the Jinn (demons), it is not impossible that a witch might decide to leave a sacrificed animal in the field. Another consideration is the level of skill involved. Many of the mutilated animals wounds showed surgical precision, and many would be far too heavy for a single person to move about, to drain its blood, or to place them in tree tops or on power lines. Having said this, let us now take a look at Satanism.

Satanism is the worship of Satan, simply put. Sources say that it is a group of religions composed of a number of ideological and philosophical beliefs and social phenomena. Of course, their shared features include the veneration of Satan. Although it seems contradictory, those Satanists who come from a Judao-Christian background often believe in much of the same things as Jews and Christians, but they choose to venerate Satan.

Satan has been known by many names worldwide. These include "Ha-Satan," which means "the opposer," and Lucifer, seen as the archenemy of our Father, therefore the epitome of evil. There are two types of Satanism. The first is **Theistic Satanism**, the second, **Atheistic Satanism**. Theistic Satanists see Satan as a real being. Atheistic Satanists see Satan as a symbol for certain traits in humankind, rather than to see him as a true being. Contemporary Satanism is mainly an American phenomena, but Satanistic philosophy has spread by the Internet and by globalization. Interestingly enough, Satanism began reaching Europe in the 1990s, with the fall of the Soviet Union, and began growing most especially in Poland, Lithuania, and predominately Roman Catholic Countries in general.[46]

To recap, then, there are two main branches: Atheistic Satanism, which includes **Le Veyan Satanism**, and **Symbolic Satanism**. Then Theistic Satanism, which includes **Lucifierianism**, the **Palladists** (which means wisdom and learning), and **Our Lady of Endor Coven**. This coven was founded in 1948 by Herbert Arthur Sloane in Toledo, Ohio, and is heavily influenced by Gnosticism, especially the book *The Gnostic Religion* by Hans Jonas. The organizations include The Church of Satan, The First Satanic

Church, The Temple of Set, and the **Order of Nine Angles**. The latter is a secretive Satanist organization mentioned in books that detail **Fascist Satanism**. This group was founded in the United Kingdom, and rose to "public note" in the 1980s and 1990s. Presently, the ONA is organized around clandestine cells called "**Traditional Nexicons**" and around what they call "**Sinister Tribes**." Another category that is given is that of "**Casual or Adolescent Satanism**." This entails teens using the Pentagram or the Sigil of Baphomet, and the trappings of a Black Mass to provide the appearance of Satanism, but it is an empty experience, that is mainly done for shock value and is not backed up by true belief. One Satanist by the name of Vexen Crabtree, states: "Satanism respects and exalts all life. Children and animals are the purest expressions of that life force, and as such are held sacred and precious." (Satanism-Religious Tolerance.org).

The Satanic Bible, written by Anton Szandor LaVey in 1969, contains the core principles of LaVeyan Satanism. It contains a number of books. In the book of Lucifier, LaVey states that a Satanist would never sacrifice a baby or an animal, as they are pure carnal beings, and thus to be considered sacred. He explains that a human sacrifice would only be accomplished to "release the Magician's wrath" during a ritual, and it would be done by curse rather than by actual murder. In a writing by Diane Vera from 2005, Ms. Vera states much the same thing as LaVey, "Under no circumstances would a Satanist sacrifice an animal or baby."

However, according to LaVey's *Satanic Bible*, if you do choose to sacrifice an animal, you should do so in a deliberately cruel manner, to maximize the animal's death throes. It is this energy that is supposed to help the spell or curse to be successful.[47] One of my contacts (who shall remain anonymous) states that masturbating or the sex act at the right moment during the casting of the spell can release the necessary energy, so animal sacrifice is not needed.

So what is to be gleaned from this information? In short, although it is frowned upon by the Satanist community, some Satanists do practice animal sacrifice, and if they are true to the methods given to them in *The Satanic Bible,* it will be with deliberate cruelty.[48] My anonymous source tells me that although he knows of some Satanists who perform animal sacrifice, he does not and he feels that the animals should not be treated cruelly. He also states that they should be eaten after the ritual, in a way similar to African Diaspora religions such as Santeria.

While it is possible that the animals they sacrifice might be left in the fields, this does not explain other signs of a cattle mutilation, such as surgical precision, and the presence of medicinal odors. Also, it would take more than one person to drop an animal into the tops of trees, as some have been found.

Some Answers

It is time now to consider the information that my Spirit Guides have given me in regards to cattle mutilations. These atrocities have been committed almost entirely by people who served and continue to serve The Darkness. This includes those who live on a number of other worlds. Some feigned friendship with our Father, while taking part in abductions and cattle mutilations. With some, it was done out of fear. They were afraid to say no to The Darkness, who often destroyed those who made him angry. Others took part because they truly were friends with The Darkness.

Why would The Darkness want cattle to be killed on our planet? That is a good question. Why would anyone want to kill any animal in such an evil and cruel way? And an even greater question: Why would they mutilate humans? This campaign began, I am told, simply as a way to demoralize and frighten us. Alien abductions also have been happening to us now for a very long time. The demoralization and humiliation of our people is only one reason for this phenomenon, and it isn't the strongest reason, either. Other reasons exist, and I will talk more about this in another chapter. However, the level of evil and cruelty involved in these mutilations leaves all people of conscience frightened and sickened. This sort of evil would have been quite bad enough, but The Darkness and the men who serve him, even to this day, did not stop with animal mutilations alone. I am told that the human mutilation case mentioned in this text occurred simply because this man fought back, trying to save his cattle. Therefore, they decided to make an example of him. This has been told to me by my Spirit Guides, as they and Father are in contact with those who own and operate such vessels. In the attempt to stop the Regatta Morte, such talks have been ongoing now for some time.

If there are unfamiliar lights in the sky, if you see something land in a country clearing one night, please resist the urge to go and see. Do not think that it is their first visit here. Do not think of yourself as a good will ambassador for our world. The threat is real and so are the cattle mutilations, human mutilations, and the abductions we have just spoken of. My advice is for you to put distance between you and the shuttle or group of men.

I am told to tell you that if they are walking, they are going to abduct someone specific, as they do not search for random abductees on foot.

They have weapons that are superior to our own, &

THEY DO NOT COME IN PEACE

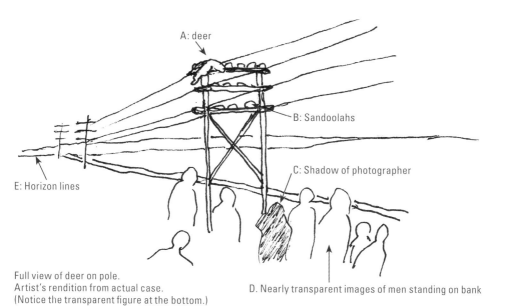

A: deer

B: Sandoolahs

C: Shadow of photographer

E: Horizon lines

Full view of deer on pole.
Artist's rendition from actual case.
(Notice the transparent figure at the bottom.)

D. Nearly transparent images of men standing on bank

Detail of Deer
(Note presence of Sandoolahs)
Deer dropped onto very tall power lines over railroad tracks.

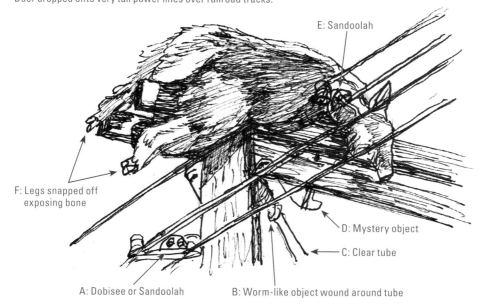

E: Sandoolah

F: Legs snapped off
exposing bone

D: Mystery object

C: Clear tube

A: Dobisee or Sandoolah

B: Worm-like object wound around tube

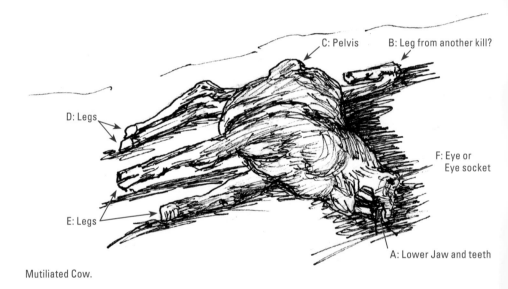

C: Pelvis

B: Leg from another kill?

D: Legs

F: Eye or
Eye socket

E: Legs

A: Lower Jaw and teeth

Mutiliated Cow.

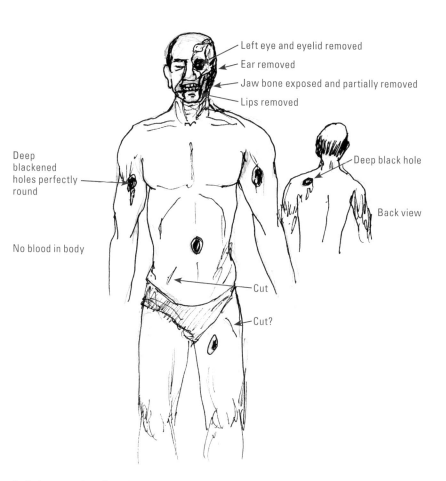

Left eye and eyelid removed

Ear removed

Jaw bone exposed and partially removed

Lips removed

Deep
blackened
holes perfectly
round

Deep black hole

Back view

No blood in body

Cut

Cut?

Artist's conception of true human mutilation case. His teeth and tongue,
as well as his scrotum were removed, and his rectum cored.
Body found at Guaraperanger Reservoir, San Paulo, Brazil.

CHAPTER FIVE

Cryptozoologica

An Exercise in Cruelty

Big Foot

In nearly every part of our world, people have heard rumors of or have actually seen creatures that appear to be an odd mixture of man and beast. There is video evidence now, and amateur groups spend nights in the woods trying to coax these creatures out into the open. As a child I can recall stories of "Big Foot" and the "Yeti," or "Abominable Snowman." At the time, we didn't take it very seriously. I know now that sightings of this creature began in the 16th century, with many of the earliest sightings reported by Native Americans. To some of them, it was known as "Sasquatch." The Sioux called him (large) "Eldest Brother," or "Chiha-Tanka." However, there have been over fifty Indian names given to this creature, depending upon the tribe, and perhaps according to what this creature looked like at the time of the sighting.[49]

During my research, I came upon an organization called Big Foot Field Researchers Organization (BFRO)." Their website is set up so that you can choose a state and find the number of sightings with specifics of the event. There are ratings of class A, B or C, according to the reliability and credibility of the witnesses involved and the circumstances, such as distance and weather conditions. Sightings can be reported to them, and presumably an investigator from that area will come and investigate. I found, much to my surprise, that my state of North Carolina has had seventy sightings from 1968 to 2012. The earliest BFRO records are from 1922 in Illinois, and the sightings have continued in every state in our country, until this time[50] (2014).

I copied the total number of sightings for each state, and adding them together; we have had over 5,487 Big Foot sightings! I urge you to recall that this is only one organization and these are the number of *reported* sightings. This says nothing about the unrecorded and unreported incidents that countless hunters and hikers must be having in the wildest areas.

In recent years, the term "Cryptozoologica" or "Cryptozoology" has come into being. According to Microsoft Word's dictionary, "Cryptozoology is the study of imaginary creatures or fabled creatures such as the Loch Ness Monster or the Yeti." However, it is personally very difficult to see these sightings as imaginary given the number of them, alone. There have been names given to these creatures, not just by Native Americans but by every group of people globally.[51]

According to "unknowncreatures.com," there have been numerous reports from non-Native Americans of seeing this creature after a UFO sighting. Soon, we will discuss the probable reason for this. It is thought that Yeti mark their territory by striking a branch against a tree, presumably to threaten unwanted guests, and they sometimes answer back when researchers strike a tree repeatedly with a branch. At this time, those who believe, see the Yeti or Big Foot as a type of bipedal primate, perhaps one that time forgot, that has existed since earlier times. This does make sense, as our wilderness is shrinking, and mankind has encroached upon the hunting grounds and territories of many animals, some to the point of extinction. Cryptozoology does not speak of Big Foot, alone. Others include the Chupacabra, Skunk Ape, Yeti, the Honey Island Swamp Monster, Cadborosaurus or "Caddie," Champ, Ebu Gogo, Batutu, Aswang, Barmanou, Chullachaqui, Batsquatch, Dover Demon, Jersey Devil, Mothman, Lizard Man, Nessie, the list is endless! Some of the descriptions overlap, and seem similar, while others seem unique.[52]

Chupacabra

Taken in order, the Chupacabra has recently been spotted in the United States. The sightings of this beast originated in Puerto Rico and then Latin America, and Mexico. The word "Chupacabra" means "goat sucker." This came as a result of goats and other farm animals being found with their blood drained out, in a way similar to cattle mutilations. The first attacks were in March of 1995, in Puerto Rico, where eight sheep were bled dry, and each had three puncture wounds in their chests.[53] In August of the same year, a woman by the name of Madelyne Tolentino saw the creature in the small town of Canovanas. There, 150 farm animals and pets were reportedly killed. In 1975, the village of Moca saw similar killings. They attributed them to "the Vampiro de Moca" or the Vampire of Moca. It was thought that these killings might have been sacrifices by a Satanic cult, but the killings continued all over the island, and each animal had three small circular incisions on their chests.[54]

A comedian by the name of Silverio Perez is known to have given the Chupacabra it's name, after the first killings. Shortly after the original killings, more deaths were reported in the Dominican Republic, Argentina, Bolivia, Chile, Colombia, Honduras, El Salvador, Nicaraqua, Panama, Peru, Brazil, Mexico, and now the United States.[55]

By now, you must be thinking that this creature alone could not be responsible for all of these killings. First of all, how could it migrate so rapidly and escape being shot or captured? After all, small animals such as rats, mice, or cats may stow away aboard ships or even aircraft, but how would a blood-eating, snarling wolf or coyote-like creature do this without being detected? Surely, there would be news of a ship's crew being killed or of this elusive animal's demise. In July of 2004, a rancher in San Antonio, Texas saw a hairless dog-like creature attacking his livestock. This was firstly labeled the "Elmendorf Beast."[56] DNA testing showed it to be a coyote with demodectic or sarcoptic mange. Two more carcasses of the same type of animal turned up in October of the same year. They also were found to have been suffering from severe mange.[57] One rancher from Coleman, Texas, reported a beast that he had trapped after losing many of his chickens and turkeys. The animal, which he described as being a mixture of hairless dog, rat, and kangaroo, was released to the Texas Parks and Wildlife officials. In an interview in 2006, the rancher was quoted as saying that this strange animal was caught on a Tuesday and thrown out in Thursday's trash.[58] With this, as is true with so many things that are unknown, apparently the authorities felt that it was best not to alarm the public.

In March of 2005, Chupacabras were reported for the first time in Russia. Apparently, farmers lost 32 turkeys which were killed and drained of blood in one night, and nearby, 30 sheep were killed and drained a short time later. The Colombia news reported that greater than 300 head of sheep had been killed in an area called Boyaca, in May of 2007, and that they had captured a possible specimen.

In August of 2008 in Texas, Brandon Riedel, a DeWitt County Deputy, reported that he observed a strange wolf-like animal—in fact it was walking in front of his vehicle and he recorded the encounter with his dashboard cam. The show *Fact or Faked, Paranormal Files* investigated this video clip and tried to debunk it, to no avail. A local farmer, who claimed to have a carcass of a suspected Chupacabra, allowed them to obtain and send a sample for DNA testing. The result? It was a hybrid between a wolf and a coyote.[59]

So is this the end of the story? No, because other questions need to be answered. Did these two animals mate on their own or is this a case of genetic tampering? If so, by whom? If this is a natural union, why or how does this predispose this creature to drinking blood instead of eating meat as it normally would? How would this animal deliver three round holes to the chests of its victims, and how would it drain a whole body by sucking alone? The more questions I ask, the more questions arise and the more certain I am that this is not done by an animal alone.

Skunk Ape

The next beast to mention is the "Skunk Ape." In most of the sightings, there were witnesses who were close enough to have described Big Foot's smell as rotten flesh, rotten eggs, outhouses, rotten fish, feces, or vomit. It has been said that the Skunk Ape is a hominid cryptid found primarily in the southeastern United States, from North Carolina to Arkansas, down to Florida.[60] The U.S. Park Service considers it to be only a myth, but reported sightings were very common in the 1960s to 1970s. In the fall of 1974, there were many sightings in Dade County, Florida in the suburbs.[61] It is seen as perhaps seven to ten feet tall, with long, tousled fur. Some reports have stated that he has red eyes. Others have said that he spreads his scent by spraying, like a skunk. This creature seems to prefer a wet humid environment, as it is often seen in southern states in and around swamps. Many think that the Skunk Ape smells bad because it hides itself in alligator lairs, with the body parts or rotten flesh of the alligator's kill. One of the more amazing photos of this animal, taken in Florida, shows him with fairly long fur and what appear to be very long arms and large ape-like hands.

There is another image of Big Foot or Skunk Ape that proved to be a hoax. I saved it on my computer so that I could enlarge it and have a closer look. When I did this, I found that several camera men were visible in the background and what looked like a rock was actually a crumpled garment bag, half opened, with a spare gorilla suit spilling out!

These creatures have been known to drop onto all fours in order to run away when fired upon. Many Cryptozoologists feel that these animals are feral primates that have evolved from abandoned pets or escaped lab animals. Some of the names that most likely refer to the Skunk Ape include "The Honey Island Swamp Monster, Fouke Monster, The Myakka Skunk Ape, Paramafee, The Green Chimp, the Holopaw Gorilla, The Abominable Swamp Slob," and "The Everglades Ape."

Cadborosaurus

Next on our list is the Cadborosaurus. Caddy, as he is called, is a sea serpent, which by description is similar in appearance to the Loch Ness Monster of Loch Ness in Scotland, Champ of Lake Champlain, and Ogopogo of Okanagan Lake, British Columbia.[62] Caddy has been spotted along the Pacific North West coast of North America. His name, Cadborosaurus, was taken from one of the places in which he was sighted: Cadboro Bay in Victoria, British Columbia.

"Caddy" has been described as a serpent with two humps or coils that are behind his horse-like head and long neck. He has a pair of fins or flippers both anterior and posterior, and the hind flippers are fused to form a large fan-like tail, which is said to provide a strong or powerful propulsion.[63] Furthermore, according to Dr. LeBlond, director of Earth and Ocean Sciences at U.B.C., and Dr. Blousfield, retired Chief Zoologist of Canadian Museum of Nature, there are no known creatures that match all of the characteristics found in over 200 to 300 sightings collected over a century.

This creature has been sighted in the last 200 years in Deep Cove, Saanich Inlet, Island View Beach, Cadboro Bay, and Saanich Peninsula in British Columbia, as well as San Francisco Bay in California. Skeptics say that a rotting Basking Shark can resemble a Plesiosaur, and in turn, Caddy can resemble a Plesiosaur as well. The Inuit Indians are painting a picture of Caddy on their canoes to keep him at bay. He is known as "**T'chain-ko**" in Sechelt mythology and "**Numkse lee Kwala**" by the Comox band of Vancouver Island, B.C. The most recent sighting occurred in 2009, when fisherman Kelly Nash filmed it with ten to fifteen young creatures in Nushagak Bay.[64]

In 2011, The Hilstrand brothers, who star as fishermen on the TV show *The Deadliest Catch* and on a subsequent show *Hilstranded*, tried unsuccessfully to find these creatures in 2011, after viewing the film taken by Kelly Nash.

Murphysboro Mud Monster

Another type of aquatic creature, or perhaps I should say another category of creature, is that of lizards and frogs, or those with a mixture of reptilian features. One such cryptid is the "Murphysboro Mud Monster." First seen in Murphysboro, Illinois in 1973, it is described as being approximately six feet tall, and of a very stocky build, covered with brown, muddy fur that has leaves and other vegetation stuck in it. It is said to be approximately 200 pounds with eyes that glow a pinkish-red color. Those close enough say that the creature has a foul stench about it.[65] He is said to emit loud growls and screams.

The first reported account involved a junk yard owner whose business was near a river. He would typically smell a foul, rotten stench just before sighting this creature as it searched for food near the junk yard. Neither one bothered the other and it would gradually lumber away, taking its foul odor with it.

In the second encounter, two coon hunters cornered the creature in an old barn. Afraid to go into the barn, one man "threw" his dog in through the doorway. The poor dog apparently howled and came running out of the barn, with the hunters quickly following!

The creature was always sighted near a river known as "The Big Muddy."[66] It is unclear, however, if this creature depended upon the river as a place to hide, to spawn, or to simply enjoy as a water source. Without this location, I would think that the Mud Monster deserved to be placed with Big Foot, rather than the frogs and lizards. After all, he is seen as having brown fur rather than scales.

Reptile-Like Creatures

In Loveland, Ohio, in 1955, three creatures were spotted by a man driving along the river at 3 a.m. They were later described as being roughly four feet in height, with green leathery skin. They walked in an upright position, appeared to have webbed feet and hands, and to this witness, each had the face of a frog.[67] The witness also stated that one of them held a device that emitted sparks. According to my Spirit Guides, this was most likely a taser or stun gun, which they would use to collect abductees. Such equipment malfunctions are common, I'm told. These were most likely not "cryptids," but Val Gorin or Zan-Besii.

In 1972, at 1 a.m., a police officer reported that he saw what he thought was a dog on the shoulder of the road. When he pulled over and shined his flashlight on it, it stood up and jumped over the guardrail and scrambled down the embankment into the Miami River. Conditions were cold and icy. The policeman described the creature as approximately four feet tall, perhaps seventy-five pounds, with leathery skin and a frog-like face. Two weeks later, the creature, or one similar, was spotted by another patrol man in the same area, but on a different road.

The next sighting took place in the state of South Carolina. It was 2 a.m., and the year was 1988. A man, Christopher Davies, was returning home from the late shift at a local restaurant. He had a flat tire and was forced to pull over. This development was responsible for an encounter that he is unlikely to ever forget! He got out of his car and changed the flat tire uneventfully. Then he heard noise coming from a nearby field. When he looked, from out of the darkness, he saw a creature running straight for him, its eyes glowing bright red! He was able to jump into his car and lock the driver side door just in the nick of time. The creature clawed at the door and window, grabbing at the handle. It then climbed onto the roof of the car and scratched and clawed at the roof of the vehicle. The man started his car and swerved to shake the creature loose from its perch! The young man, who was, needless to say, very shaken, told his parents about his encounter. A check of his car revealed deep scratches and marks on the roof, and the driver side mirror was broken. The description of the lizard man is as follows: he is able to walk in an upright position. The creature stands approximately seven to eight feet tall, with red glowing eyes, and is covered with green scaly skin. The head and face are said to look like a cross between a human and a snake, with a center ridge from the top of the head to the snout. He has three fingers with long black claws on each.[68]

Mr. Davies passed a polygraph test, in regards to this incident. Several large, three-toed footprints were found in the area. This was in Bishopville, South Carolina, near the Scape Ore Swamp.[69]

The most recent report was made in 2004. The creature was accused of attacking a young girl and trying to pull her into the river.

The Loveland Frog and Lizard man are not the only two cases known. In Native American mythology, a race of lizard men existed in the Carolinas before the coming of the white man. The area was known to them as "Inzignanin."[70] This term means roughly a " place to fish," and its inhabitants were often called "fish people."

I am told by my Shamanic Spirit Guide that it was seen as a place to go if you wished to become one of them. When anyone went there, they never returned, and it was assumed that they had joined that tribe. The "**Shawnahooc**" or River Demon known to the Shawnee Indians, and the "**Mamnegishi**" of the Cree Indians of Eastern Canada are tales or legends told about similar creatures.

In 1974, in Wayne, New Jersey, a man spotted a large green humanoid with "large frog-like eyes" and a wide lipless mouth cross the road in front of his car. This was near White Meadow Lake. In August of 1972, a group of young men were chased away from the banks of Thetis Lake by a creature who was covered with scales. One of them had lacerations on his arm, and he believed that the creature had put them there during the chase. Two more witnesses had an encounter four days later in the Thetis Lake region. Russell Van Nice and Michael Gold reported that the creature rose up out of the water, looked around and then disappeared back into the lake.[71] In November of 1968, in Riverside, California, Mr. Charles Wetzel reported that he had been attacked by a large scale-covered humanoid, that had large eyes, a disproportionately large head and spines protruding from the back of its head. Mr. Wetzel had been driving by the Santa Ana River at the time. He further stated that the creature had attacked his car, leaving long scratches in his windshield. A second witness came forward, and said that the same or similar creature had jumped from bushes along the roadside and into the path of his car.[72]

In April of 1977, in Dover, Massachusetts, a man by the name of Bill Bartlett was driving home with two of his friends in the vehicle. In his headlights, he saw a small figure moving slowly along a roadside wall. The figure was three to four feet high, hairless with a large head, no nose, elongated limbs, and it had large, orange eyes.[73] Two hours later, another young man had a similar encounter. Fifteen-year-old John Baxter was walking home from his girlfriend's house, when he saw someone walking along the road. He called out, thinking it to be someone he knew. The figure then stopped, darted down one side of the gully and up the far side bank! Baxter tried to follow it and reportedly got a good look. He stated that it had a big head, and a very thin, long body. He then became afraid and fled. Since that time, the creature has been known as the "Dover Demon."[74]

Shapeshifters

Skin Walker

Although they are not really seen as cryptids, I wish to include Skin Walkers in our discussion. They are reputed to be human shapeshifters, who can transform themselves at will. This term originated in the southwestern United States, and has figured prominently in Native American myths and legends. According to Navajo belief, a Skin Walker is a type of witch, one that is so very evil, that part of his/her initiation into the world of this craft is that of killing a close relative, or sibling. The Navajo name for the Skin Walker is "yee naaldlooshii" or "with it, he goes on all fours."[75]

Male Skin Walkers are far more prominent than females, and it is said that only childless women can become Skin Walkers. They are most likely to assume the shape of a coyote, wolf, owl, fox, or crow, but technically, they can assume the shape of any animal they choose. It is believed that they can take the shape of or "steal the skin of" another human as well. If you lock eyes with one, they can "absorb themselves" into your body.

They are usually described as naked, with just an animal skin. Some

Navajos describe them as a mutated version of the animal they wish to become. They are known to break into the house of their victims and attack the people there. They may bang on the doors, the windows, and the roof. They have been known to attack cars in this way, causing the driver to have an accident. They are thought to have the power to read our thoughts and to make any human or animal noise that they want. This might include the cry of a baby or the voice of a relative, in order to trick the victim into opening their doors and walking outside.[76] The skin walkers are said to use charms as a part of their magic: human bone beads, shot with blowguns so that they lodge under the victims skin without leaving a mark, and human bone powder or dust, which causes paralysis and heart failure. Such things as the victim's hair wrapped around a potsherd, and placed in a tarantula's hole, or in a rattlesnake's lair is said to be a part of their evil sorcery. This sounds very familiar, much like the black magic we have already talked about, which came to the U.S.A. from Africa and the islands. Recall the "zombie dust" that was formulated from many poisons and blown in the face of their victim, paralyzing them in a way similar to the drug Curare.

It has been noted that when a victim is trying to fire upon the Skin Walker, their weapon will jam until it makes its escape. After this, the gun will work without a problem. It is also said that if they are running away, there will be no footprints, and if fired upon at point blank range, the bullet will have no effect. The Navajo also believe that the only way to kill a Skin Walker is to dip the bullets into white ash.[77] This is very reminiscent of the types of powers possessed by the Bat-winged Ones or the Bretheren. It is my personal belief that some of these abilities are really the Bat-winged Ones traveling with the Skin Walker and helping them to do such things as crying with the voice of a baby (which they can do). Also, the Bretheren can travel in other sub-dimensions, thus leaving no foot print in ours. They can fly as well, but the Skin Walker? They may find it possible only if they shapeshift into a bird. Even the jamming of a gun might be done by the Bretheren.

The Navajo believe that the Anasazi were responsible for much of the witchcraft in the Navajo community, including Skin Walkers. Therefore, Anasazi ruins and graves are considered taboo.[78] I have no proof, of course, but am told by my Spirit Guides that the Anasazi people were, in 2005, found to be trapped in a sub-dimension that had no other life in it, save for them. It is thought that they were placed there by Satan, but this is not known for certain. However, it explains why they disappeared, with food uneaten on plates, and cooking vessels and baskets left behind: a very abrupt departure. What is certain is that Satan would have had the technology to do this to them. Why this was done, I do not know, but our Father rescued them and they are now home on Parutia.

I am also told by my Spirit Guides that there are only three humanoids known who can or could truly and completely shapeshift into an animal—our Father, The Darkness, and Satan. Could this ability be given to a witch that the evil ones wish to reward? Yes, possibly. Others who claim to do this may be just projecting their consciousness to an animal, and "riding along" with them. This is called remote viewing. It is possible to do this, but I am told that most animals do not like to be used in this way, and it can frighten them badly. Therefore, it is best not to do it.

The Doobisee

There is one known group of people who are naturally born as shapeshifters. They are called The Doobisee, as mentioned earlier. Smart and fast, they are human souls, but are not humanoid in appearance. It is believed that they are a very ancient race from some area far from Earth and also far from Parutia in the 5th dimension. They were experimented upon genetically by The Darkness, and then brought to many different planets in the 5th dimension and to Mars, our Moon, and Earth, in the third. They possess the ability to change their appearance from a cute little dog-like creature, to that of someone who resembles a vampire bat, but their body is not quite the same shape as that. In the photos that I have taken for the last fifteen years on battlefields, as well as in my own back yard and home, I have captured them in many different configurations and it never ceases to amaze me how well they can camouflage themselves. At times, they can be translucent, and blend with each other to form barricades to prevent me from taking photos of objects. They can blend themselves into the background, and look like trees or stones. They can move between sub-dimensions and even

travel in space. They are, in short, amazingly and wondrously made. The problem comes with the way in which the Doobisee must live. As I have stated, they are Vampires who must drink human blood in order to survive. They were primarily interested in animal blood, and lived in nature and in harmony with it, that is, they did not over-graze or kill off the animals they fed upon. Originally, they lived a happy existence out of doors, drinking animal blood, as well as eating some vegetables and fruits. However, The Darkness changed them into vampires who must drink human blood to survive. This need is all encompassing for them and they can easily kill those whose bodies they enter, by over feeding.

The Darkness tampered with them genetically, so that they would kill off all of Father's children, and many of his own. His plan was working until this was recently discovered and now they are being helped to return to their former lives in the wild. One of the ways in which they were discovered was by the Doobisee attacking space ships. They have the ability to move through solid objects by changing their sub-dimension, which they can do at will. This method is used also to keep them hidden, as they become invisible to us. They have been attacking space ships by infiltrating the vessel, and then gradually feeding upon all of the inhabitants one by one. I am told that this is quite different from their original and true nature and every effort is being made to restore them to their true selves, so that they can live once again in harmony with mankind and animals.

Why not exterminate them? Because they are human souls, who were created in this way and they have lived for a very long time as Doobisee. They lived in peace and harmony. How many people can say that?

However, the fact that they must now drink human blood is serious enough at this time to classify it as **a sixth planetary emergency**, adding it to the five planetary emergencies outlined in my first book *To Help Lost Souls Find Home*. Anyone who finds themselves suffering with anemia of unknown origin, or sudden weakness or pallor should ask their Spirit Guides for help and ask Father in prayer to check them for such a problem. Then a trip to your own physician is very important if you have such symptoms. The Doobisee favor those with high blood sugars, so it is especially important for diabetics to see a doctor if they suspect anemia, or if your blood sugars are staying higher than normal and you feel weak and tired. Also, those who suddenly find themselves craving sugar as they never have before may need to have their iron checked as well. The Doobisee are very good at urging a victim subliminally to "sweeten their blood" before they attack. With the cravings, the person might hear mentally: "Something sweet is good to eat!" Although many Doobisee are returning to the 5th dimension, there are still enough of them here to create a danger to our health. **I must also state that I am not a doctor and I do not intend this as medical advice or treatment of any kind. All such advice should come only from a licensed healthcare provider.**

Ebu Gogo

Our search for cryptids now takes us to a creature known as the Ebu Gogo. Roughly translated "Ebu" means "Grandmother" and "Gogo" means "who eats anything," in the Flores language of Indonesia. These people are thought to have existed not so long ago. Their legend continues on amongst the Nage people and it is difficult to separate the truth from the fiction. According to the Nage, the Ebu Gogo were still alive in the 17th century, and there are some people that contend that they existed until the 20th century, but are no longer seen. The Nage believe that the Ebu Gogo were hunted down until extinction by the Nage people in the Flores region of Indonesia. It is said that the Ebu Gogo stole food from human dwellings, and kidnapped their children. Apparently, after one child was kidnapped and eaten, the villagers decided to trick the Ebu Gogo into accepting gifts of palm fiber for their clothes.

When the Ebu Gogo took the palm fibers into their cave, the villagers threw in a fire brand to set the cave on fire. The tale says that all were killed except perhaps one pair that still to this day live somewhere in the deepest forest areas.

According to the Nage people, the Ebu Gogo had wide flat noses, broad faces, with a large mouth, and a hairy body. The females were said to have long, pendulous breasts. They were said to be very fast runners and good walkers, who were between three-and-one-half to four feet tall. They reportedly murmured in what was perhaps their own language and would repeat what was said to them in a parrot-like fashion.

There is an article published in *New Scientist*, (Vol. 186, No. 2504) that reveals similar information, and to this day, such stories are even being told on YouTube. Gregory Forth, Professor of Anthropology at the University of Alberta, Canada has investigated their linguistic and ritualistic roots and has stated that the stories of the Ebu Gogo, or "Homo Floresiensis" may be rooted in fact. The remains of a three-foot tall hominid, which was given this name and existed as long as 13,000 years ago has inspired much speculation.[79]

But the question is this: Who were these people, really? Given what we know of the biodiversity of our world, it is likely that they are or were survivors of a small colony. They were most likely sent here to establish a colony without Father's knowledge and then ran into many dangers. Like the Resilva of Easter Island, they may have been sent with virtually no weapons in hopes that Satan and his men and The Darkness and his followers would see them as a non-threat and worthless to their needs. Expensive equipment and weapons would have tempted Satan and the others to at least raid their new colony, if not destroy it outright. It is also possible that these people fled from a raid in another area entirely and somehow made their way to Flores. Perhaps they reverted to the cave and lost most of the knowledge that they would have had regarding their home. Many such colonies, as I have said earlier, became extinct when war destroyed their homeland and the supply ships simply never returned.[80]

Bat-like Creatures

The next category of cryptids we need to touch upon is that of the bat-like creatures. The Leeds Devil (also known as the Jersey Devil), Mothman, Batsquash, the Rakshasa of India, the Batutu and the Aswang of the Philippines, the Snallygaster, and Springheel Jack are a few of the names given to these creatures.

Leeds Devil

Let us begin with the Leeds Devil. The Leeds Devil, or **The Jersey Devil**, first appeared in the 1700s, in an area of New Jersey called The Pine Barrens. This is an area of forest land that is large enough to hold the state of Rhode Island, and it contains swamps and has been left undeveloped, for the most part.

According to the New Jersey Historical Society, there are several versions of the story. Perhaps the most popular began in the 1700s. A young woman by the name of Deborah Smith emigrated from England to America to become the bride of a Mr. Leeds. The Leeds family resided in the area known as the Pine Barrens. (Today, the location is noted as Leeds Point, Galloway Township, Atlantic County, New Jersey.) It is said that she bore Mr. Leeds twelve children. When she discovered that she was about to give birth to their thirteenth child, it is at this point that the stories differ. In one, she calls upon the Devil during her painful labor. After she gives birth to her child, it turns into a devil and flies off. In another telling, she is a Quaker who refused to be converted to Mr. Leeds's faith. The Minister, frustrated at her refusal, tells her that her thirteenth child will be the child of the devil. In yet another version, it is said that it was the product of a Leeds family curse. In one version, she yells after hearing the news that she is pregnant again with her thirteenth child, "May it be a devil!" Another states that she cared for her devil child until her death. At that time, he flew into the woods![81]

One thing is known for sure: witchcraft was widely believed in the 1700s, and a deformed child was seen as being the child of the devil or as a sign that the child had been cursed by God. This might be as punishment for the sins of the parents or the child might be seen as evil.[82] Because Mr. Daniel Leeds served as Deputy to the Colonial Governor of New York and New Jersey, it is possible that the stories were conjured up (no pun intended) in an attempt to destroy his political career.[83]

This legend was a fairly obscure one until a rash of sightings in 1909 prompted the newspapers to publish information about them. At that time, one account described the Jersey Devil as having leathery bat wings. It also said that it had the body of a serpent, the head of a horse, with cloven hooves, two small arms, a devil's forked tail, and a horrifying screech.

The truth is that there have been thousands of sightings since the 18th century. Here then are a few:

1. Commodore Stephen Decatur saw a flying creature while he inspected the making of cannonballs at the Hanover Mill Works. It was flapping its wings and was not affected when he shot it point blank with a cannonball!

2. In 1820, Joseph Bonaparte, eldest brother of Napoleon Bonaparte, witnessed the Leeds Devil while hunting on his estate in Bordentown.

3. In 1925, in Greenwich, Connecticut, a farmer found the corpse of an unidentified creature. He showed it to 100 people, and none could say what it was.

4. In 1937, in Downington, Pennsylvania, some boys claimed to have seen the Leeds Devil during "Phenominal Week." It was also spotted in Gibbstown, Pennsylvania at that time. Phenominal Week was, I am assuming, a holiday created for the enjoyment of the townsfolk, who were mostly comprised of those who did not believe in the existence of the Jersey Devil.

5. In 1957, there were claims that a corpse matching the Leeds Devils description was found.

6. In 1960, reportedly, loud shrieks were heard around May's Landing. Merchants in Camden, Massachusetts offered a $10,000 reward for the capture of the Leeds Devil, and they also offered to build a small private zoo to house it in.

7. In 2008, over ten encounters were reported to the local "Devil Hunter's Group," according to the New York Times.[84]

Mothman

Our next creature is known as Mothman. The sightings of Mothman occurred in November 15th, 1967. On November 16th of 1967, the *Point Pleasant Register* published an article with the headline "Couples see man-sized bird." In 1975, John Keel wrote the book *The Mothman Prophecies*, and introduced Mothman to a much wider audience. In his book, he puts forth the idea that the appearance of the Mothman coincided with a number of disastrous events, including the collapse of the Silver Bridge, in West Virginia. For those interested, there is a film of Mr. Keel's book also, called *The Mothman Prophecies*. It was released in 2002, starring Richard Gere.

But what happened on November 15, 1967? Rodger and Linda Scarberry and Steven and Mary Mallette told police that they saw a large white creature whose eyes glowed red when the car lights hit them. One described the eyes as being reflective and red. They described it as being like a flying human with a ten-foot wing span! It began following their car when they passed by an old WWII munitions factory. Two volunteer firemen saw it as well. They saw "a large bird with red eyes." A contractor by the name of Newell Partridge told Sheriff Johnson that when he aimed his flashlight at the creature in a nearby field, its eyes "glowed like bicycle reflectors." He reportedly blamed a buzzing sound coming from his television set and the disappearance of his German Shepherd on the Mothman as well.[85]

Wildlife Biologist Dr. Robert L. Smith at West Virginia University told reporters that the descriptions all fit the Sandhill Crane, which is a large bird, almost as large as a man. This crane has a wingspan of seven feet, and has red circles around its eyes.

Sadly, there were some hoaxes that the authorities had to deal with, as well. In one, construction workers tied red flashlights to helium balloons, hoping, perhaps, to add to the confusion. A folklorist, Jan Harold Brunvand, noted that 100 people had reported seeing Mothman, and that most likely, many more saw him without reporting their experience.

But what kind of prophecies did this mysterious man make? John Keel, in his book states that prior to the collapse of the Silver Bridge in December 15, 1967, a number of predictions were made. These prophesies came to the people who had seen the Mothman and foretold disasters worldwide, with the destruction of the Silver Bridge being the last prediction made. Ufologist

Jerome Clark stated that members of the Ohio UFO Investigators League re-interviewed several people that were originally interviewed by John Keel himself. All of them claimed that the testimony they gave was completely true, and many said that they had seen the Mothman since then.[86]

The original sightings were interwoven with these predictions, as well as UFO sightings, lights in the sky, disturbances of electric appliances, such as TVs and telephones, visits of the mysterious "Men in Black," which were most likely FBI Agents. Because of the predictions that later were proven to be true, many in the area see the Mothman as being a good creature, one who tried to help the residents of that small community, during difficult times.[87]

The truth of such things can often be less appealing than the legends. I am told that the Mothman is not a single being. However, how many of them inhabit the TNT area of West Virginia it is difficult to say. In fact, now that the area is being monitored, it is possible that they have left altogether. The Mothman actually is one of the humans altered both genetically, surgically and chemically by The Darkness to create a unique killing force for his armies. They call themselves "The Bretheren," or the Valdurii (Valiant Ones), that we have discussed earlier. The fact that they were and have recently been seen around the abandoned TNT factory suggests that they are using that property for some purpose. It is entirely possible that the whole thing began when they decided to chase cars and harass people who lived in close proximity to the factory and adjacent woodlands, probably in an attempt to frighten them away.

The German Shepherd that disappeared was probably seen as a nuisance that would bark and sound the alarm as they would come and go from the site. But why would they have need of an old abandoned factory? Recall, if you will, that they often use a drug similar to Curare to immobilize their victims. Such places would already have labs and some lab equipment in place. They can travel between sub-dimensions and so even if a lab is still being used by us, they could set their lab up in the very same room as ours! They would simply find a sub-dimension in which there was no one there. I realize that sounds incredible, but it is true.

When there is a haunting in which people complain of hearing voices, such as two people having a conversation, or hearing doors opening and closing, or furniture being moved about, this can be the reason. It does not even need to be the Valdurii, it can be people who live naturally in a sub-dimension that we are for some reason able to hear. In the fifteen years that I have been doing this work, I have found that the Valdurii do gravitate toward empty buildings as a place to work or to use as a staging area. Empty secret tunnels provide them with unseen highways so that they can move about unseen by our Guardians.

But why the predictions and prophecies? This I do not know. As a guess, I would say that they did this to frighten away people who lived or traveled around that site. The publicity, however, did the opposite. I am told that the demise of the Silver Bridge was caused by them.

Perhaps they thought that it would keep out tourists and thrill seekers. Perhaps they thought to make us believe that they were helping us by giving us a glimpse of the future.

Whatever their reason, I am told at this time that it is a fact that the Valduri Batui or the Bat-winged Ones did indeed destroy the Silver Bridge. Knowing this, it is also understandable that they could make those predictions, because they were the ones who created the disasters that they predicted in the first place! Another purpose that the old TNT factory might serve is as a place to bring abductees to await pick up, to be taken by shuttle to a larger spaceship. This is one very good reason why we should consider destroying old buildings that have been empty for a while and cost a lot to renovate. They can easily be put to use by the Valdurii and the Jinn (or out-of-body demons), as well as alien visitors who may use them as a holding area for those who are being abducted.

Batsquatch

The next cryptid to discuss is the "Batsquatch." As the name implies, this creature is bat-like. The Batsquatch is described as seven to eight feet in height, with purple skin and red eyes. It has a wide wingspan and his wings are leathery like a bat's and has been sighted around Mount St. Helens and Mount Shasta.

Why hide around the rocks of that area? It is possible that those volcanic mountains are dormant in other sub-dimensions, and that they are living or manufacturing the drugs they use in old lava tubes underground.

In several accounts, the Batsquatch is described as a flying primate, with Pterodactyl wings.[88] I am told by my Spirit Guides that there exists on Parutia a Pterodactyl-like bird that has been given a portion of land to minimize human interference, but it is gradually becoming extinct. It is possible that such a bird has been introduced into our environment. If this is so, it would have been done by those who served The Darkness and the Children of the Night (they have no connection with the Earth organization of that name), who serve the darkness, while living here in our world. Our people would not do this, as having such a predator suddenly introduced into a fragile ecosystem could cause other breeds to become extinct. Also, they are very dangerous to humans and can disembowel a man with one swipe of their talons, which have sharp

spurs like those of the dinosaurs.

It would not look bat-like in its face, however; so this can be ruled out. There are a small number of Bretheren that had their skin turn purple, or green instead of brown or black, during the chemical, genetic, and surgical process that they were forced to endure. Because they often had very pointed faces due to fat pads of their faces solidifying and they wear a goatee which emphasizes this, it is much more likely that the Batsquatchs are simply Valdurii. I have been told, and it bears repeating, that the Valdurii were created as an elite force of assassins in The Darkness's army. Therefore, likening them to a simian or primate is inaccurate. Despite what has been done to them, they are human souls in those bodies—human souls who need Father's help and forgiveness.

Aswang

Our next cryptid is the Aswang. The Aswang is described as an evil vampire creature that resides in the Philippines. The Spanish that colonized the Philippine Islands in the 16th century understood the Aswang to be the most feared of all of their mythological creatures.[89] Interestingly, this myth is well known through out the Philippines, except for an area called Iloco, that does not have an equivalent myth or story. However, they have a creature called "Irene E." (Could this be a neighbor no one cared for?) This myth is popular in the Western Visayan region, such as Capiz. Aswang, according to some, is a catch-all term, used to describe all kinds of witches, vampires, manananggals, shapeshifters, therianthropes, and other monsters. It is the monster who steals and eats the cadaver and leaves behind dried banana trunks in its stead.[90]

Aswang legends vary greatly region to region, but most say the Aswang are female in gender. The original definition means "eater of the dead." The Aswang legends were used as a way to understand and to explain such things as miscarriages, before modern medicine. In fact, even to this day, Aswang stories are very popular and are favored by the tabloids and their readers. This is especially true when ever there is a grave robbery or a child kidnapping. People with peculiar or strange habits are often suspect.

The Vasayan region of the Philippines is replete with Aswang stories, and is said to be an area of high paranormal activity. Therefore, many people of that region are very superstitious. They decorate their homes with garlic and holy water, and pregnancy is seen as a time of vulnerability for the woman, who fears that the Aswang might take her child. Some stories say that the Aswang live amongst the villagers during the day as shy reclusive people. At night, they shapeshift into an animal—a dog, or pig, cat, or bird—and then kill and eat unborn fetuses, especially liking the heart and liver. Some are said to have long proboscises, which they use to suck the fetus out of its mother. Recall, if you will, that there is a rare type of Valduri or Bretheren, who has a beetle-like face and a proboscis. They are called the Valduri Karnak and are said to be very fast and silent. One type of Aswang called the Bubuu, makes the sound "of a hen laying an egg at midnight." We can only guess what that might sound like! They replace a stolen cadaver with a banana trunk, or they may send in a facsimile or copy of that person who was kidnapped. This copy will then return to the victims home, but then will become sick and die.[91]

Aswangs are said to have bloodshot eyes from staying up all night searching for houses with wakes, so they can steal the cadaver. Interestingly enough, a film was shot that was titled *Aswang: A Journey Into Myth*. It was written by Jordan Clark and distributed by High Banks Entertainment, Ltd. I am not certain if this is still the case, but the proceeds of the film were to be used to help restore power to Olotayan Island, Roxas City, and help support people who suffer from Dystonia Parkinsonism. Capiz has the highest rate of this disease, at 21.94 per 100,000 cases, or one for every 4,000 men. Aklan has the second highest, at 7.72 per 100,000 cases. Some believe that Dystonia was the origin of the Aswang stories, because some of the symptoms of Dystonia resemble the characteristics of the Aswang. Short clips of the film may be viewed on YouTube. It may be possible to order a DVD from High Banks Entertainment, Ltd.

Rakshasa

The next cryptid to address is the Rakshasa. The Rakshasa is a mythological being who is known by a number of names: in Sanskrit, *Rakshasa*, in Tibetan, *Srin Po*, in Malay and Indonesian, *Raksasa*, in Assamese, *Raikhox*, in Bangla, *Rakkhosh*, in Chinese, *Loucha*, in Japanese, *Rasetsuten*. As these variations imply, they have traveled and existed within a wide area. In Hindu and Buddhist faiths, they are seen as unrighteous or evil spirits. The Ramayana states that they originated from Brahman's foot. Hinduism maintains that the Rakshasa are particularly evil persons in previous incarnations. They are notorious for disturbing sacrifices, desecrating graves, harassing priests, possessing humans, and other demon-like activity. Their fingernails are said to be venomous, and they are said to feed upon human flesh and spoiled food.[92]

Recall, if you will, that the Bretheren carry a mixture of viruses and bacteria that are toxic. A scratch or "bite" causes systemic gangrene that destroys from within by lysing the red blood cells very rapidly. To survive, one would need immediate transfusions and huge doses of anti-viral agents. The black patches that form on the organs of the victim would have to continually be removed as well. I have been told by a survivor in the 5th dimension that it felt as though their blood was boiling as soon as the virus entered their blood stream.

The Rakshasas are also known as shapeshifters and magicians. In Hindu and Buddhist writings and holy books, there are stories of many

Rakshasa, some good and some evil. They are generally known as giants, who are strong, and monster-like in appearance.

It is time to separate fact from fiction! The Rakshasa are none other than the Bretheren in all likelihood. They have very brown to black skin, and they can certainly admit growls and imitate voices as previously discussed. They are not shapeshifters as such, but they can shrink down in order to fit inside a human host, or if hiding, they may do this to fit into a confined area. They can render themselves invisible by switching sub-dimensions, which allows them to pass through solid objects such as walls and they have large leathery bat-like wings, as well. They do not eat rotting flesh, however. (There are a people called **The Jahartha**, who do this. The Jahartha have been among us a very long time. They are not children of The Darkness, but they did serve him. They can be seen in funeral parlors, battlefields, and anywhere else where dead bodies are found. Without them, we would be inundated by slowly decomposing bodies. This is their function, and they do this by agreement with Father.)

Snallygaster

Our next cryptid is called the Snallygaster. This creature was first sighted between the 1800s to 1932, in the mountainous region of western Maryland. It is described as a half-bird, half-reptile, with a ghoulish face. Its beak appeared to be very strong, almost metal-like, with very sharp teeth. Those who witnessed the Snallygaster said that it made shrill and screeching sounds, similar to a large bird. The name comes from the German "schnelle geist," or "fast ghost-spirit."[93]

In the early 19th century, reports of this creature increased, and it was said that it lurked in barns and stole chickens. There were also reports that it tried to attack people and damaged their properties. The people of that area in Maryland began painting seven-pointed stars on their roof tops, windows, and barns to ward off this frightening creature.

The first person to say that he had seen the Snallygaster was James Harding. Mr. Harding claimed that the creature only had one eye in the middle of its forehead and made shrill noises as it flapped its wings. He described it as looking like the cross between a vampire and a tiger![94]

Snallygaster hunts became popular, much as Big Foot hunts and ghost hunts are today. The Smithsonian Institute offered a reward to anyone who caught the beast. In 1932, amid nervous, panicky townspeople, the Snallygaster was declared dead. Revenue Agents George Dansforth and Charles Cushwa saw the dead beast in a vat of moonshine whisky, during a raid. A "shadowy photo" was published in the newspapers. Reportedly, the agents blew up the still and destroyed the carcass before an autopsy could be performed. It was supposed that the creature was attracted to the smell of the mash, and circled it, inhaling fumes until it passed out.

Springheel Jack

Our final cryptid to discuss goes by the name of "Springheel Jack." Jack has been witnessed since 1837 to the present day. He has been sighted in London, England, Silver City, New Mexico, Cape Cod, Massachusetts, and Santa Fe, Argentina. Jack is described as a tall, thin man, wearing a dark cape and a close-fitting cloth helmet or a hat. His hands have large claws and his eyes glow a bright red at times. Witnesses have stated that he has an acrid odor to him.[95]

In 1837, a woman testified that she heard a loud knocking on her door, and when she opened it, a man was standing there. She took this man to be a police officer. He shouted, "For God's sake, bring me a light, we have caught Springheel Jack in the lane!" She went to fetch a candle and when she returned, the man was gone. She ventured outside and saw a man at her gate. As she gave him the candle, he removed his cloak and spewed blue and white flames from his mouth! The man then began tearing at the woman's dress, scratching her face and stomach. The woman's sister heard her screams and the man ran away just as her sister approached.[96]

After the 1800s, he was no longer spotted in England. By the 1930s, he was sighted in the U.S.A. and Argentina. Other witnesses also reported that he spewed blue and white flames from his mouth, and one claimed that a bullet passed right through, without causing him damage. In 2005, the year in which he was last seen, he was described as wearing black clothing that included a cape and a balaclava (a ski mask). As in previous sightings, his eyes were said to glow a bright red. It was also observed that he could jump from rooftop to rooftop, taking leaps that could be five meters high and ten meters long.

It is possible that this creature may have actually been a synthetic human—an android. This explains the metal beak, and the blue and white flames. However, how he could have been made to jump so far is hard to say. I am told that androids weigh in excess of 500 pounds and are not athletic!

In the 5th dimension, we do have the ability to create synthetic humans, but they can't move about with such agility, I am told. It is possible that a Bretheren may have posed as a Springheel Jack, because they are far more agile.

Another Possibility

There is another possibility that we have yet to discuss. Volumes could be written about all of the cryptids reported and catalogued worldwide. Here, we have only discussed and described a few. Generally, they seem to fall within several types: ape-like, sea monsters, amphibian-type or frogmen, crocodilian, and lizard like, bird-like, and bat-like creatures. Others may be dog or wolf-like in appearance, and still others have been described as Otter-like. We have also mentioned that The Darkness did create children who were Crocodilian in nature, a Crocodilian head, with a very strong stocky human body—the Val Gorin. He also created Those who were lizard-like in appearance—the Zan Besii. However, he created many others.

One such group, **The Dragoon-sah** (*drah-goon-SAH*), are a very small and very straight and thin people who, by report, have had many problems with their backs and their gait. Their ability to bend and flex was hampered by their design.

There is another group of surgically altered humans called The Zerkah. **The Zerkah** (*zer-KAH*) are human souls and human in appearance, but they have totally white skin, black eyes—that is, the sclera or white of their eyes are tinted black—and they are made to look like white marble statues. They often hide in forested areas and rise up from their "graves" when they are summoned. Like the Valduri, they can drink only small amounts of blood and are not required to feed, unless ordered to do so by their high command. They can fly as all of the Valduri do, without wings. Only the Valduri Batui have true wings. It is thought that The Darkness created the Zerkah to look like Roman or Grecian statues because our Father chose the Roman-style togas and other clothing and architecture for our government. On Parutia (Heaven) these are still being used out of respect for tradition. The Angels continue to wear tunics and sandals and the leaders of our Guardians wear helmets that are very Roman in appearance. Archangel Michael has often been depicted wearing this type of helmet by artists in our world.

The Dragoon-sah were seen, probably for the first time nationally when *Fact or Faked—Paranormal Files* ran a segment in which a man sent in a film clip from his home security system. On camera, he saw these stick-like beings in long coats that conformed snuggly to their bodies, marching across his lawn en route to his house. They were also the subject of inquiry when the same type of being peered around a bedroom door, and realizing that he was on camera, fled.

Another group of The Darkness's followers are called "**Lucifer's Children**." As I have mentioned earlier in this text, these are Draconians who were indeed created by our Father. After leaving Parutia, they pledged themselves to

The Darkness, who gave them red skin and horns and asked that the men all wear black goatees to make them appear more devil-like. There also exists a group of his children called "**The Nimble Ones**" or "**The Renunciata**" or "**The Renunciates**."

The Renunciates are thin, very flexible, and able to scale great heights, and do aerial maneuvers that would impress the toughest circus critic. What their true function is, I do not know at this time, but it is fascinating to think that many of The Darkness's children might very well be responsible for the folklore of Faeries and wee people!

I also have no doubt that there are other groups that prefer to remain unknown to us. Many of the children of The Darkness and many of those who were his allies actually cooperated out fear rather than love or admiration for him. No doubt there are others that may never come forward, and also many who have succumbed to the "Evil Madness" or the Druxsella 7.0 virus spoken of earlier and in my first book.

The home planet of the Renunciata has been decimated by this horrible plague. All upon that planet are now gone. I am told that they, as a people, met their death with courage and grace. Those who were left at the end met and sat in a circle, meditating and chanting until their end. "Renunciata" means those who renounce the teachings of our Father. However, they were a peaceful and spiritual people at heart. I was allowed by my Spirit Guides to speak briefly to one of their leaders, at that sad time. I was given permission by them to use their photos in this book. I was allowed to listen as they chanted, swaying in unison, crying softly. They met death in peace instead of panic and violence, which is the way most planets have ended. I have a huge admiration for them.

The Cryptids' Connection to Father

Before drawing this chapter to a close, there is one last point to be made. As the title of this chapter suggests, Cryptozoologica is indeed an exercise in cruelty. In our 5th dimension, there have been many who have chosen to follow The Darkness instead of our Father. Some have done this out of fear of retaliation from The Darkness and his followers. They knew that Father would forgive them, and would not retaliate if they began serving The Darkness, but the reverse was not true. Many bad things came out of these alliances. Genetically modified bacteria and viruses—of which the Druxsella 7.0 is one—larger and more deadly warheads, many different ways to hurt, maim, or kill the human body, many different machines and methods also. Satan himself helped to design the Druxsella virus, I am told. The Flesh Desiccating Sensors that I spoke of in the first book are but one invention that Satan helped to bring about (more about this later). Genetic tampering and experimentation also has been a huge problem. It has been outlawed, but elicit research continues on. Often such labs or "hospitals" are located in mining communities in remote areas. Many mining communities are domed communities on large asteroids or small planets that would be otherwise uninhabitable. With these labs or research communities well hidden, they continue by using abductees from many worlds, including ours, to work the mines.

By now, you must surely be wondering what this has to do with cryptids. When those who serve evil abduct someone who is a friend or a child of Father, someone who serves him as part of the Parutian Government and often Guardians that have been abducted while working with one of us here on Earth, those who serve evil are now capable of transferring all of that poor person's soul from their own body to that of a genetically altered and created "monster." Then they set them loose on Earth in remote areas to fend for themselves. Those who retain their memories of who they are and where they came from have to learn how to hunt and kill animals and eat raw meat, and this is doubly offensive because many of Fathers children are vegetarian. Those who do not retain any of their memories may actually have it easier, and may be able to survive a short while. I am told that the longest my Spirit Guides have heard of one surviving was six years. That particular case involved the "Mermaid" seen off the coast of Israel, several years ago. She had forgotten who she was and had adapted to her life in the sea, but was curious about humans and would have eventually been captured, and possibly dissected. Father helped her to return home. She'd spent six years of lonely isolation and often in very cold climates.

I am also told that probably ninety-eight percent of the cryptids we have discussed have human souls within them. The latest news that I have heard in regards to this, is that they (those serving evil) are now sending cryptids such as Big Foot with a female partner, so that they will reproduce in the wild. Any viable offspring would be animal, not human. Therefore, any cryptid with memories intact, will be raising animal children, not human, which has got to be punishment in its own right. Therefore, the cruelty is evident on all sides. The animal that the human is put into has lost its life, their bodies have been modified to be different than other animals on Earth, and are probably a composite of a number of animals. The human who has his or her memories intact suffers loneliness and isolation as well as the hardship of living outside with the elements. The number of sightings a year in my country alone speaks volumes in terms of the seriousness of this problem. We do not need hunting parties of Big Foot thrill seekers rambling through the forests, looking to "bag us a 'squatch." Try to remember that a human soul may be hidden within that massive body. A soul that has known our Father. A soul who needs understanding and love. Don't expect that he will passively come to you. Some people, by report, have been hurt when they have come upon a Yeti in the wild. However, it is possible that he may understand if you talk to him. Most animals are fairly telepathic. Many are also intelligent enough to converse with, by telepathy, or by visualization. If spotted, tell your Spirit Guides immediately, so that Father can help them, and do not attempt to cage them or fire upon them. This is the most compassionate thing that you can do.

"Yeti" or "Big Foot.
" 7-10 feet tall

Silver Bridge collapse.
Possibly destroyed by
the Valduri (Bretheren),
then called "Mothman."
West Virginia.

Detail from under a bush near author's home.

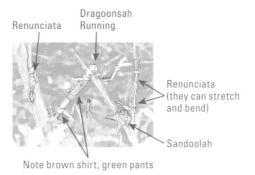

Renunciata

Dragoonsah Running

Renunciata (they can stretch and bend)

Sandoolah

Note brown shirt, green pants

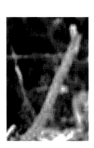

Dragoonsah leaning on a wall, right front.

Sandoolahs

Luciferian (Draconian)

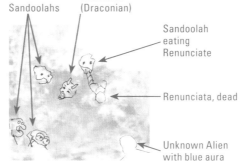

Sandoolah eating Renunciate

Renunciata, dead

Unknown Alien with blue aura

Luciferian

They are trudging through tall grass, in front of other larger people in The Darkness's forces.

Small Ninja-clad humanoids that are true vampires

Light aliens unknown

Doobisee   Sandoolah

Mining Colony. Temporary enclosure? Note many men inside at least three looking my way (as I was shooting the photo). Many blurry faces in the foreground—Doobisee and robots.

Many different people at colony. Temporary transparent work area?

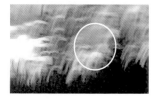

Note small people

Egalatarians
Men—Eagle Heads

Mining colony. Eagalitarians emerging from the light and others.

More men arriving at mining colony.

Raven Rock, North Carolina.

Rennuciata—pony trail through trees.

Hazy area is the transporter energy. They are literally "beaming up."

Sandoolah

Sandoolah eating Rennuciata (see feet and shoes)

Transporter beam   Original full view, Bull Run

This is a detail from Bull Run Battlefield in Northern Virginia.

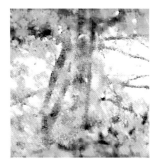

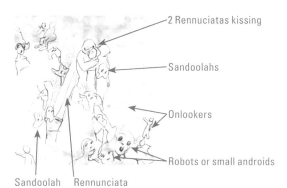

2 Rennuciatas kissing

Sandoolahs

Onlookers

Robots or small androids

This was taken at Bull Run in Manassas, Virginia.

Sandoolah   Rennunciata

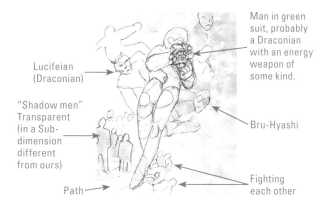

Man in green suit, probably a Draconian with an energy weapon of some kind.

Lucifeian (Draconian)

"Shadow men" Transparent (in a Sub-dimension different from ours)

Bru-Hyashi

Path

Fighting each other

A Luciferian.
Raven Rock, North Carolina.

These are samples of writings received during an automatic writing session. Sign reads "no Admittance!" or "Halt! Do Not Enter!" in five languages according to my guides.

CHAPTER SIX
Regatta Morte
The Death Ships

Fifteen years ago, when my awakening began, I had no concept of where it would lead. I only knew that if my Father, our Father, called me, I would not say no to him. I was told that I had a Sacred Contract, an agreement that I signed before coming to Earth in this lifetime. I was to become a minister, and to help the souls around us to return home to Parutia, or Heaven. I was to find a way to teach this to others. They gave to me the standardized method that I now use and teach, which I call "Spirit Releasement."

However, in this fifteen-year period, much has taken place in the 5th dimension, as well as here on Earth. My ministry changed from one of reconciliation and love to that of messenger. It has become my sad task to deliver bad news to all of my brothers and sisters on Earth. Now that I have expanded and completed the knowledge of the first book (*To Help Lost Souls Find Home*), it is time to show how all of these facts are interrelated.

As the title of this chapter suggests, you are about to hear of "The Regatta Morte," or death ships. The Darkness, after leaving Parutia, traveled extensively and did a very good job of winning the inhabitants of other worlds over to his way of thinking. Those he did not win either cooperated or died. No doubt, many worlds cooperated out of fear of retribution. He created many of his own children such as the Val Gorin, and he also kidnapped children of Father and placed them upon planets that were very distant, often in other dimensions. They gradually saw The Darkness as their creator, and were faithful to him.

The Darkness was not a whole man. He was a genius, as is our Father, but his hatred spawned many bad things. One of the worst was "The Regatta Morte." The worlds of the 5th dimension have reached the point of exhausting their mineral and rare Earth stores and fossil fuels. Higher technology means greater dependence upon electricity and other types of energy. Many devices run on atomic power there, even small handheld devices. Therefore, the need for uranium, plutonium, and other minerals are always in demand. Once one becomes dependent upon such technology, it is very difficult to let go of it to conserve power and resources. Mining colonies sprung up on small planets, and on large asteroids. Most of these are contained under a dome because they have little or no atmosphere. I am told that even planets that had been destroyed by war and were still highly radioactive have held mining colonies because the need is so great! The Regatta Morte abducts people from many worlds, sometimes at random, and some times for political reasons. The Abductees are tortured both physically and mentally and they are then killed. They have the technology to retain their souls, and they are traded for the minerals needed to keep their society running. They are sold into slave labor in mining colonies after being put into stronger, genetically modified bodies so they can work. Others may be experimented upon. It is an evil, cruel practice set in motion by the Darkness. Gradually, it is coming, at last, to an end. But why torture? Ultimately, evil does not need a reason. Let us hope that once this horrible injustice comes to an end, never again will man seek to subjugate his brother for any reason. There is no reason great enough to justify cruelty.

Unfortunately, what is also true is that these mining colonies have also hosted such things as illegal research facilities that experimented on humans, most if not all supplied by abductions. Illegal genetic research is something that The Darkness

supports, because Father is against it, and because it is often inhumane. Because he hated Father and his children so very much, he was inhumane to them whenever possible.

Of course it is also true that, as a genius, research of any kind interested him. He and his men were always finding new ways to destroy the human body and to find newer and more horrible weapons. It is also true that Satani (or Satan, as we say here) was also genius in so far as research and genetics is concerned. He worked along side other scientists to develop many horrible devices. One of those is the Flesh Desiccating Sensors we spoke of earlier. One or two of these microscopic devices implanted into a person can cause a fatal chain reaction that literally liquefies the entire body. It is thought that many of us on Earth now have these sensors, without knowing it. It takes a certain set of frequencies to begin the process and such devices as the MRIs could potentially set the sensors off. MRIs work by using not only the very strong energy of the magnet but also a series of radio signals. If the right combination is given or if enough energy is given by the magnet alone, it could be fatal, should the Flesh Desiccating Sensors be present. Even Reiki, which emit's a particular frequency of healing energy, has been shown to cause the sensors to become "excited," and Reiki is no longer being channeled by us as a result. It is simply too dangerous. Other healing modalities are safe, such as Healing Touch, which manipulates the subject's own aura, rather than channeling a different frequency of energy. Toning by voice is safe, but tuning forks are not a good idea, either. But why would any of us have these devices in us? I must once again remind you that we also have a huge problem with the genetically modified virus called the Druxsella 7.0, also called "The Evil Madness." This is because at the onset of the illness, the patient becomes confused and then often very mad and violent or evil. As it runs its course, organ systems fail and the subject dies. Without any kind of treatment, the patient can last only a few months. In that time, they can infect countless others. *This nightmare is spreadable by all vectors!* During the death throes of some of the planets, the military have implanted these microscopic devices into many people, at random. Those who run mad can also develop paranoia; this has led to random killing. They possess a technology in the 5th dimension that can reach into other dimensions, and can be used to hurt others even at a vast distance. It is by that technology that such things can be done to us, without our knowledge.

It is known that there have been some animals in remote places that have contracted this disease, or have been given it; and therefore, it is not *if* but *when* we begin to contract this illness. Father wants desperately for us to begin making plans to deal with the virus. It is hoped that a cure or treatment will be found by the time it emerges on Earth.

But what of the Regatta Morte? It is thought that this idea was in its infancy during the time that the Mayans and the Nazcas were colonizing Earth. Recall that I stated that the dead, those sacrificed by their own tribe, were discovered in the area of the Nazca lines. It is my belief that when the spacemen came and used those landing strips now called the Nazca Lines, they were viewed as gods. In all likelihood, they commanded that these sacrifices be made before they traded with and resupplied the Nazcas. The souls of these sacrificed people would then be collected and held aboard the ships. Yes, they had the technology needed to do this, even back then. It may also be true that other people from many other colonies on Earth were killed and their souls collected in order to have enough souls to trade for the minerals they needed from the mining colonies.

Eventually, this evolved into a terrible business, a slave trade. These ships would travel not only to Earth, but to many other inhabited planets in the 5th dimension and beyond. The souls they stole were kept in a containment unit, and once brought to a mining colony, they were transferred to genetically modified bodies and put to work in the mines. Some would remember who they were and where they were from, but most probably remembered nothing of their past. They would be worked to death, basically.

Cryptids, such as Big Foot and the others, have been found by Father to be human souls who have been abducted and then sent to Earth to live as an animal, in those modified bodies. I am told that there is a great effort to get all of these souls home to Parutia or to the Universe, which is where we go from Parutia (or Heaven) when our physical bodies die.

Unfortunately, this is not the end of the story. Gradually, The Darkness and his followers decided that in order to make more obedient and passive workers, their wills had to be broken. Thus, these ships became ships of horror, in a Hitler-esque fashion, and were designed to torture those abducted, while still in their bodies—atrocities beyond description, out-fitted like a gymnasium from Hell. Once the individual died, the soul would be contained and sold to the mines. It is thought that this began in the 1700s, but we do not know for certain, according to my Spirit Guides.

On Parutia, Father was not made aware of this nightmare until the 1800s! There have been many problems involved in closing down these death ships. They are often in areas not completely covered legally, therefore, laws have to be made by intergalactic counsels, many of which are or were sympathetic to The Darkness. One commander killed himself recently, when he found out that his own grandmother, who had disappeared years before, had died aboard one of the ships he had been defending while talking about this issue with Father.

Most of the people who are abducted are killed. However, some have been abducted, tortured, and then sent back to their beds at home with no memory of having been aboard a ship. The same technology that can put sensors in us can also be used to heal many if not all of the wounds so that the abductee has no idea of what he or she has been put through, after returning home. Sometimes, the Guardians of the abductees are taken also and I have been told that over eighteen of my own Guardians have been abducted over the course of my 57 years. Others have been found to be disloyal to Father. One evening, I found myself sketching very rapidly, a phrase in several different languages, none of which are from this world. This proved to be a memory from an abduction. It was a warning sign written in several different languages. I recall running my hand over it during one abduction, in an attempt to figure out where I had been taken.

As I talked with my Spirit Guides and began my awakening, memories returned of a dual life, a life of having been abducted and tortured every three years, since I was 16 months old. This was done in a way that kept Father from knowing about it, as hard to believe as that is. Only a few memories have surfaced, but they have been bad enough that I'd rather not remember more. However, my Spirit Guides have helped me through this process and I simply let the memories wash over me, like the dirty spray from the wheels of a truck in mud—and I emerge shaken, soiled, but not defeated.

This has been the case for many upon this world, and others. It is very likely now that these death ships may soon be a thing of the past. It has been a difficult process, as so many worlds are dependent upon those mines, and the mines have become dependent also on this disgraceful slave labor. Many of these mines have closed or have been destroyed, by war or by accidents such as malfunctions of life support systems. Many of the planets that tolerated, manned, and supported these ships are gone due to war or the Druxsella 7.0, many of the mines also.

I am told to emphasize that the Regatta is in the process of ending. Earlier, it was not possible for Father alone to end this disgrace, because so many worlds were refusing to change. To keep these ships away from us would have meant all-out war with many worlds, simultaneously. Earth and our homeland would have been destroyed in a heartbeat! Then why should I talk about this at all? I have chosen to because there have been approximately six times more alien ships in orbit around Earth than would normally be here. They are unhappy with Father and desperate for the minerals that they need. They can hide from us easily by moving into sub-dimensions just out of our ability to see or detect. Unfortunately, this unhappiness with Father, Earth, and Parutia could still lead to war, or it could lead to a bid to invade Earth. Now more than ever, it is time for us to awaken to who we are, where we are from, and why we are here! Once we can hear our Spirit Guides and Father, we can be given updated information and guidance in the days ahead. We must side with what is right, and we must be very sure of how we feel.

It is very possible that the Servants of the Night and the men aboard these death ships might walk among us, trying to down talk our Father, trying subtly at first to win us over to their side. The affects that they (The Darkness and his followers) have had on us in our media and our thinking shows that this brainwashing has already begun in small ways. Take a look at the American diet, as one example. A few decades ago, we were learning to reduce the amount of fat and salt in our diets. Alcohol and caffeine also were supposed to be things that responsible adults must curb, to live longer. Now, you have only to pick up one woman's magazine (I will not mention the name) to see the affects they are having on us: recipes for mixed drinks, strong ones, that are candy flavored to help the next generation to imbibe, chocolate and candy suddenly are good for you! Cream and butter are now back in most of the recipes, also. And here are other amazements: bacon is being put on cakes, and salt granules are on everything, including chocolate and caramel. I have even seen a recipe in one magazine for ice cream with bacon in it! Obesity is rampant in our country, but we are supposed to unwind with a large swig of alcohol and bacon ice cream? Also, even more disturbing are recipes for cupcakes, puddings, or other treats that attract our children are now being spiked with *dreamsicle*-flavored vodka ! A few years back, cigarette and alcohol ads were removed from television to try to protect our children. Have we not noticed that they are all back on TV and in magazines? More and more, people are developing high blood pressure. They are finding it in very young children. They are eating too much salt and fat and sitting too long at computers and televisions. We have a responsibility to our youngsters to keep them safe and to try to set a better example than that.

It is no mistake that this is happening. Our thinking and media are being affected. Even the sudden craving for something else that is not good for us: four- to five-inch high heels! In another year or so, someone should do a study to see how many women, mostly young women, will have crippling foot ailments due to wearing these! As a nurse, I have seen women who have had to have surgery to be able to put their heels down on the floor again, because their Achilles tendons actually shortened, and bunions, too, almost certainly will increase. I advise us all to keep our eyes open to the signs of the times.

The small amount of truth that I have given you will surely be corrupted and used to try to win over as many children of Father as possible, in the days ahead. While it is true that our world and all the people upon it are not perfect, we, as children of Father, must try our best to remain on the side of what is right and decent. Our amnesia is now a luxury that we can no longer afford.

Conclusion

We have come full circle. I have given you a few very interesting and very unsettling facts regarding the 5th Dimension, and of our home land, Parutia. I have spoken about how these facts affect us here on Earth in the third. Hopefully this has brought you a bit closer to your own awakening. From time to time, I hear someone say "he speaks his own truth." What is true and real is factual and remains the same. What varies from person to person is our own interpretation or understanding of that truth. This, of course, is colored by our own life experiences and our individual level of understanding at that point in time. This can change as we grow, learn, and become. That is what awakening is, soul growth. We grow to the point of no longer being afraid to question and to understand; we do this by asking our Spirit Guides and by learning from them as well as reading, meditating, and prayer. Once we reach our awakened state, we become the enlightened souls that our Father wishes us to be. It also signals that our maturity has helped us to be strong enough to accept the facts in this matter, even when those facts are not pleasant.

We are children of one Father, all of us on Earth. It is time to love one another and to work toward lasting peace. Our world has between 75 and 100 years left, possibly less. We should all strive to use this time to make our Father proud of us. We should seek to shelter and protect the young and the weak, and to work, all of us, toward the highest good in all of our affairs. **But again, a word of caution:** If there are unfamiliar lights in the sky, if you see something land in a country clearing one night, please resist the urge to go and see. Do not think that it is their first visit here. Do not think of yourself as a goodwill ambassador for our world. The threat is real and so are the cattle mutilations and the abductions of which we have just spoken.

My advice is for you to put distance between you and the shuttle or group of "men." I am told to tell you that if they are walking, they are going to abduct someone specific, as they do not search for random abductees on foot. They have weapons that are superior to our own, and:

THEY DO NOT COME IN PEACE

Glossary of Terms

Angels

Men and women created by Father before mankind was brought into the physical. They were created as our military and law enforcement on Parutia, as well as being stationed in other governmental jobs, such as our Guardians and Spirit Guides.

Angelorium=male angels, Angeloria=female angels. The Angeloria often work in teaching positions, and healthcare. They differ from ordinary men in that they are all blonde-haired and blue-eyed, very pale. They also have a deeper sense of emotions and are educated with a greater emphasis on spirituality. Most of them live with Father in the palace, but a few live in private homes or apartments. They are all raised and educated in the palace. At 16 years of age, they receive fully functioning wings, and are instructed how to fly.

African Diaspora and the Seven African Powers

This refers to the time when the slave trade of various European nations displaced huge numbers of Africans, placing them as slaves through North America, South America, The Caribbean, as well as Europe. Many African-based religions believe in the seven African powers, or deities: Ellegua, Obatala, Chango, Oggun, Orunla, Yemaya, Oshun, Baba-Lu-Aye, Aquanyu-Sola, and Oya. These religions sprouted in the locations where these people were enslaved, often mixing with Catholicism, as well as other religions. The names of the Christian saints were given to the seven powers, so that the slaves could worship their own deities and practice their own religion, without this being understood by their owners. Slaves were often forced to be baptized before working in their owners homes, without any instruction in the Christian faith.

Aliens

People or beings who are not born upon the Earth, but instead have traveled here. We, ourselves, are not native to Earth. We represent the second attempt to colonize Earth. The first was Atlantis.

Aspect

This refers to a small part of each person's soul, which is separated by Father from our higher selves, so that we can be born on Earth and live in multiple lifetimes. In this way, we can all be here on Earth in more than one lifetime at the same time, and our higher self is still back home on Parutia, working as usual. We are returned to our higher selves when we leave our bodies and return home via the inter-dimensional corridor, or light. In this way, approximately 3,000 souls are peopling the entire planet!

Astral Plane

A sub-dimension that our consciousness travels to when we sleep, both on Earth and on Parutia (Heaven). This is the dream plane, where we process all that happens in our wakened state. It is possible for our Spirit Guides to give us dreams during this time. It is also possible for the evil ones to give us nightmares during this time. Regard them as "junk mail."

Astral Projection

The ability to project one's consciousness outside of the body, not into the astral plane, but while awake, into the 4th dimension. Our Spirit Guides can help us with the process, but it is not safe to do this, especially not by ourselves! The Jinn may be around and can stop us from getting back into our bodies, which would lead to our physical death in twenty to thirty minutes.

Atlantis

This refers to the first colonization attempt made by Father after the experiment with the dinosaurs and the Ice Age. It was a small agricultural community located in the Mediterranean region, in the area that is today the Mediterranean Sea.

Aura

This refers to the energy of our soul, which extends out from us on all sides approximately five feet. The frequency of our soul's energy is referred to by its color. This, in turn, reflects the spiritual and emotional maturity of that person on a soul level. It can also indicate illness, which can be revealed in this way before it is evident in the physical layer in many cases.

Awakening

The state in which we as humans know and begin to understand who we are, where we are from, and why we are here. At this point, we can access past-life information more readily and can have spontaneous recall of past lives, and even of our life on Parutia (Heaven). It is important for all of us to begin our awakening process so that we can have the help, the wisdom, strength, and advice of Father and our Spirit Guides in the troubled days ahead.

"Bad One"

This is a casual term referring to the Jinn, or any evil or infected soul. This can also be used to refer to the Valdurii.

"Bat-Winged Ones"

This is a term used to refer to the Valduri Batui or "Valiant Bats." This can also be used to refer to all other Valdurii: V. Lupei, V. Skelatti, V. Karnak, V. Gorin, V. Loratui, as well as V. Corpus Void.

Biodiversity

This refers to the wide variety of peoples, cultures, plants, and animals upon our world.

Bodhisattiva

These are souls who have finished their Karmic Cycle or Karmic Obligation and choose to return as teachers, prophets, and mature souls to help our people grow spiritually at a faster rate.

Bokor

(See also "Capalata")

A Bokor is a practitioner of black magic in the Vodun religion.

Bretheren

This refers to The Sacred Order of the Bretheren, or the Valdurii (see Bat-winged Ones.)

Bru-Hoi

Children of The Darkness, with large, almond-shaped eyes, heart-shaped faces, and green to gray tinted skin, small build, short statue, the "Roswell Aliens." Their name means "Brave Warriors."

Bru-Hyashi

Children of The Darkness, a branch of the Bru-Hoi, their name means "Brave Army." They are of larger build, taller, and their faces are more elongated.

Cassiopeia

The name of the star constellation where our homeland, our home planet is located. We are a planet called Parutia, which orbits the third star in Cassiopeia. It is a twin star. On Earth, most of us still regard our home as Heaven. Parutia exists in the 5th dimension, not the 3rd, which is where our Earth is located.

Capalata
(see also "Bokor")

These are practitioners of black magic in the Vodun religion.

Chakras

These are energy centers which spread our life force energy to all of our organs and cells of our bodies. They can be affected by our upbringing: trials of life, emotions, and illnesses. They must be harmonically balanced for optimum health. When a chakra is out of balance, it can lead eventually to illness in the physical body.

Cosmic Consciousness

This is a collective group of souls from which all of us have been taken in order to live on Parutia in the physical world. Human life in all dimensions throughout the universe comes from this collective of souls. Animal souls have their own group and their own collective place where they return to and live happily, apart from man. However, animals return to Parutia from Earth.

Creator

Father, on Parutia created us, chose how we look, and many more particulars about our selves. He was charged with bringing us into the physical world and teaching us, but he did not create our souls. Our souls come from another collective within the Universe and our Universal Father creates our souls.

Created Children

Although The Darkness did bring into the physical many children, he also created a number of children that were originally human in appearance. The Bretheren are one such example. These were human males whose appearance and physical abilities were altered biologically, chemically, surgically, and genetically. It is believed that the Slevessii Selveii were also created (created, not born).

Cryptozoology

The study of imaginary creatures according to one dictionary. However, numerous sightings have led many of us to believe that they do indeed exist. These are such creatures as Big Foot, the Yeti, etc. In many cases, it has been found that the evil ones or those who serve evil in other dimensions, have created genetically modified bodies and placed the souls of humans into these bodies and dropped them into wilderness areas of our planet. This has been done as a cruelty and a political move to punish those who serve Father. When they can be located, Father brings them back home to him.

The Darkness

When being brought into the physical world, Father's energy split unevenly during a "post induction shift."

This resulted in Father with 60% of his souls' energy and The Darkness, with 40%. The Darkness seemed to be the embodiment of evil without conscience or the normal impulse controls. Neither wanted the other back, and he remained separate until several years ago, when they were finally reunited. However, his reign of terror continues, the battle between good and evil still very active.

Demons

These were humans or people from other planets as well who vowed to serve The Darkness. They traveled to Earth out of body and their energy was altered to be more frightening in appearance. This can be a donkey, a troll with pointed ears, a pig, and others. One such demon appears as a skeleton wearing a black robe, like the "grim reaper," but without a scythe. These are the Generals of their army. They are also called "Spiritui Morte" or "Death Spirits." The Spiritu Morte "are out-of-body and are not to be confused with the Bretheren, or Valdurii, who can travel between sub-dimensions and be invisible or solid. The Demons are called "The Jinn," collectively.

Doobisee

These are people who at one time were living peacefully in a far-off land, living as vegetarians. They were found by The Darkness and genetically modified to be vampires in the truest sense. After this change, they have followed The Darkness, as part of his army. They are human souls, but they do not look human. They are shapeshifters also, and can travel between sub-dimensions and even into space, which makes them a danger to space ships because they can breach a ship's hull and walk through, without setting off an alarm. They exist on Earth, Mars, Parutia, and other planets as well.

Draco Constellation

This is the Dragon constellation. The Draconians originated from a planet in this constellation. In their colonies here on Earth, they used the dragon symbol in their art and they built pyramids that aligned with the stars, particularly their home constellation in the 5th dimension. The Nazca lines are one very good example.

Dragoon-sah

These are a branch of The Darkness' children. They are very small, with very straight backs, white skin, and small, short arms and legs, which makes moving about and lifting difficult for them. Their heads can't move at all, I'm told. They are human souls from the same place as our own, but were brought into the physical world by The Darkness, not our Father.

Earth Changes

For a number of decades, channels and clairvoyants have predicted a time when the Earth would ascend to another dimension, and we would then be all awakened, ascended beings. There would be marked signs: strong storms and other natural disasters, such as earthquakes, rising water levels, and the possibility of Earth being knocked off of its axis by a meteor, and a greater loss of life. This was to be followed by a long time of peace and a rise in consciousness and spirituality. A number of prophecies touch upon this, including the Mayan calendar, the Hopi and the "I AM America Map."

End Of Days

The end of days is spoken of in Revelations—the Armageddon, the four horses of the apocalypse. This was to be preceded by signs such as a blood-red moon, seas boiling and turning to blood, and fire raining down from the sky. There is to be much fighting and violence, and a whole generation of souls used as "cannon fodder." This would then be followed by death, disease, and finally, judgement. Although it may not happen this way, we are in the end of our days upon Earth. Father believes that we may have less than 70 years before our world becomes unlivable.

Energy Body

Our souls each contain many layers or bodies of energy. Each layer has sub-layers—very complex! Basically, we have a Mental, Emotional, a Spiritual, and a Physical layer of energy. Our physical layer or energy body is a type of energy called "Standing Wave Energy."

Flesh Desiccating Sensors

A horrible invention created by Satan and other scientists as a doomsday weapon. They are microscopic sensors that when stimulated with a specific frequency of energy, cause a chain reaction which liquefies the human body, usually very rapidly. It leaves behind a pinkish-tan liquid as well as dental work (metals), artificial joints, etc. Countless people have died as a result of this nightmare invention, since its conception. Because so many infected people, often in the military, have put these sensors into unsuspecting targets both on Earth and elsewhere, including the 5th dimension, Reiki has been taken from us and is no longer safe for the practitioner or the client. It is no longer advisable to have MRIs which use a strong magnetic field in conjunction with radio signals. TENS units may also be dangerous. Here on Earth, we do not have the technology to remove or even see the sensors, unless it is posthumously, with an electron microscope. (This is one of the five planetary emergencies spoken of in my first book.)

Imprint

An imprint is an image left behind after a violent and wrongful death. This differs from a place memory, which does not have to be of something violent or unpleasant. This can be like a film clip of something repetitive, such as children playing in a school yard. However, these can also be of such things as a murder, though, playing the act over and over.

Inter-dimensional Corridor

This is the tunnel of light so frequently spoken of. It is by this light, or "Wormhole" that we return to our world of Parutia. The journey may also be taken by space ship, but due to the sheer number of souls on Earth, it would be impractical and very costly to send us home in this manner. We must be out of body in order to travel home by the light.

Palo Mayombe

This is the dark side of Santeria. It originated in the African Congo and is considered to be the most feared and most powerful form of Black Magic. Those who practice are called "Paleros." It was spread with the slave trade to Cuba and Puerto Rico in the 1500s. Its influence can be felt in Central America: Brazil and Mexico. Santeria calls upon the forces of good, whereas Palo Mayombe calls upon the forces of evil or darkness. It has its own rules, its own priesthood. It is said that practitioners of Santeria avoid the practitioners of Palo Mayombe.

Postmortem Bloat

This is the filling of the abdomen and organs, such as the stomach and intestines, with gases, a by product of bacterial proliferation. This can force stomach contents and blood out of the mouth of a corpse and it can lead to the abdomen opening up or bursting. This is one of the things looked at to determine the cause of animal or human mutilation.

Regatta Morte

This means "Death Fleet." These are ships that are outfitted with torture equipment of all kinds, as well as a containment unit which can hold human souls up to a year. The abductees are tortured to death, and their very souls stolen and placed in the containment unit. Some abductees may be placed back into their beds, with no knowledge of what was done to them. Others, who are lucky enough to be returned, may regain bits and pieces of their experience. The rest will die. Once the ship meets its quota, the souls are taken to a mining colony and exchanged for ore or minerals. This meets the needs of the mining colony for workers, as they are placed into a genetically modified body, and are then strong enough to work. The ships travel to our dimension and the 5th dimension, and most likely others, abducting people.

Remote Viewing

The ability to project ones consciousness to a designated place, and "to see" what is or has taken place there.

Shapeshifting

The ability to actually change the physical layer of our energy to appear as something else, such as a wolf or a raven. It is my personal belief that in Native American Spirituality, shapeshifting refers to projecting one's consciousness into a living animal, such as a bird, in the same way as remote viewing, rather than changing shape. I am told that only Father, The Darkness, and Satan were able to actually change shape. By remote viewing it is still possible to see briefly through the eyes of an animal, but I have been told not to try this as it frightens the animal, and might even hurt them.

Santeria

A complex of religious cults (Cuban, the way of the saints) in the Afro-Cuban population, combining Yoruba African and Spanish Catholic traditions, especially concerning the saints who are identified with the spirits or "Orishas" of the Yoruban Pantheon. Each worshipper may have a personal patron saint and belong to a group or congregation under a priest. It involves rituals, animal sacrifice, trance possession, and the Orishas. Worship features prayer, song, and drumming. *M. Gonzales-Wippler,* The Santeria Experience *1982, and* Rituals and Spells of Santeria, *1984* A priest is called a Santero (male) or Santera (female).

Skin Walkers

In Native American Spirituality, a Skin Walker is a very evil and powerful witch or warlock, who has the ability to shapeshift into animals, imitate the appearance and voice of others, and many other frightening abilities. The Native American name is "Yee Naaldlooshi," which translates into: "With it, he goes on all fours."

Slevessi Selvee and Slevess Signat

The names mean "The Shameless Ones." They were (most, if not all, are now gone) three feet tall, white skin, and the sclera of their eyes were very brown to black. They had brown to black hair and the men and women looked a lot alike. The men wore a goatee. They were vampires in the true sense and had to feed on human blood. Created, not born, they were unable to mate, I am told. They fed by shrinking down, and entering the body by shifting into another sub-dimension, and opening a spot by using a small blade. Another branch of them was called "Slevess Signat." They were smaller and clean shaven, and looked a bit troll like. They had red eyes. They, also, are gone now.

Spiritui Morte

These are the Generals or high ranking warriors of The Darkness' army here on Earth. They are human souls, children of Father, who have either been forced, brain-washed, or willingly taken into his service and then have become leaders within it. Their appearance has been altered energetically to appear as a skeleton wearing a black robe with a hood or cowl. They are here out of body, and many no longer have bodies to return to, due to war and/or the decimation of various planets by the Druxsella 7.0 .

Solar Desiccation

The effects of the sun on a corpse. It causes the break down of all exposed tissues and hastens bacterial growth and bloat. This is something that is looked at in regard to mutilations.

Spirit Releasement

This is the method given to me by my Spirit Guides, so that I could help souls to return home. I was told to teach it to anyone who is interested in doing this work. My Spirit Guides hope that this simple method will eventually take the place of all of the home-made rituals that we have used here on Earth, when trying to help the souls return home. This method works with Heaven and it helps a rather large group of souls to return at any one time. If you are truly serious about helping our ancestors to return home, your Spirit Guides will work with you, but this method helps them to help you and is what they wish us to use.

UFOs

This stands for "Unidentified Flying Objects." Most of us today understand that this really means a space ship of unknown origin. Unfortunately, this often is a death ship of the Regatta, looking for abductees; they may also intend simply to frighten us by appearing over a crowded city or over a highway, for instance.—a show of force. Many, if not all, of the Regatta are also equipped to be fully functioning battleships, I am told. Their weapons are superior to ours, as their technology is beyond ours.

The Universe

A vast vacuum, a place filled with planets and stars, and other heavenly bodies.

Our Universal Father

Our Father on Parutia made our bodies, but our souls come from a great collective of souls, even beyond the Cosmic Consciousness. Our Universal Father created our souls, and possibly created all of the universe as well.

Zan-Besii

These are lizard-like in appearance and may be behind sightings of lizard-like men on our planet. These are children of The Darkness—not created, but born. They have snake-like eye slits, where as the Val Gorin usually have round pupils. Like the Val Gorin, they have to eat raw meat. Their name means "Fierce Lizards."

Endnotes

Chapter Two

1. "The Tasks of The Wise Man." *The World Religions*, 2nd ed. by Ninian Smart (Cambridge University Press,Cambridge Mass. 1998) pg. 188

2. Excerpt from *The World Religions*, 2nd. ed. by Ninian Smart (Cambridge University Press, Cambridge, MA. 1998) pg. 188-191

Chapter Three

3a. "Peru-Facts (http://peru-facts.co.uk/nazca lines.html) pg.1

3b. Sacred Tree of the Ancient Maya (http://maxwellinstitute.byu. edu/publications/jbms/?vol=6&num=1&id=133) 8/1/2012, pg. 1-11; The Mayan World Tree (http://www.awarenessmag. com/julaug07/ja07_mayan_world.htm), pg. 1-4; "Place of the Standing Stones." *National Geographic Magazine* (http://ngm. nationalgeographic.com/ngm/0405/feature4/) pg. 1-3, May 2004

3c. Ibid.

4. "Sacred Destinations (http:www.sacred-destinations.com/peru/ nazca-lines) pg. 1-2,

5. "Place of the Standing Stones." *National Geographic Magazine* (http://ngm.nationalgeographic.com/ngm/0405/feature4/) pg. 1-3

6. Sitchin,Zacharia. "Ancient Astronauts." Wikipedia (http:// en.wikipedia.org/wiki/Ancient_Astronauts) pg. 4; "Ancient Aliens"(http://www.history.com/shows/ancient-aliens.History. com) 06-04-2011

7. The Aetherius Society (http://www.aetherius.org/the-mother-earth/atlantis-lemuria-maldek) offical site; Atherius Society. Wikipedia (http://en.wikipedia.org/wiki/UFO_religion)pg. 1-2

8. The Church of the Sub-Genius. Official site (http://www. subgenius.com)

9. Heaven's Gate (http://heavensgate.com/misc/intro.htm) Official site; Heaven's Gate (Wikipedia (http://en.wikipedia.org/wiki/ UFO _religion)

10. Industrial Church of the New World Comforter (Ibid.),pg. 2-3, Allen Michael (http://wwwgalactic.org/Allen Michael/pdf)

11. Nation of Islam (http://en.wikipedia.org/wiki/UFO religion) pg. 1-2

12. Raelism (Ibid.) pg. 1-2; Raelism. Official site (http:// usa.rael.org)

13. Scientology (http://www.scientology.org) Official site; Hubbard, L. Ron, *Scientology: A New Slant on Life*, 2007 (Los Angeles, CA, Bridge Publications, Inc.) pg. 25-26, 295-343, *The Oxford Dictionary of World Religions*, 1997 (Oxford,NY, Oxford University Press) pg. 869

13a. Ibid.

14. Unarius Academy of Science (http://www.unarius.org) Official site

15. The Universe People (www.ashtarcommandandcrew.net/profiles/blogs/cosmic-people-of-light-powers); The Universe People (http://en.wikipedia.org/wiki/UFO religion)

15a. Ibid.

15b. Ibid.

16. Tempelhofgeselschaft (Ibid.) pg. 18.

17. Judaculla Rock (shadowbox.brinkster.net/judaculla.html); Judaculla Rock (Stonepages.com/news/archives), Jan. 2004

Chapter Four

18. Fort, Charles. Wikipedia (http://en.wikipedia.org/wiki/Charles_Fort) pg. 3-11; Cattle mutilations (http://en.wikipedia.org/wiki/Cattle_mutilation) pg. 2-14

19. Ibid.

20. Ibid.

21. Regarding John Altschuler. Wikipedia (http://en.wikipedia.org/wiki/Cattle_mutilation) pg. 3

22. Ibid., pg. 3

23. Ibid., pg. 3

24. Human mutilation (http://www.think-about-it.com/mutilations/Human_Mutilations.htm) pg. 16-19

25. Mutilations, Characteristics of. Wikipedia (http://en.wikipedia.org/wiki/Cattle_Mutilation.htm) pg. 4-5

26. Lab values (Ibid.) pg. 4-5

27. Properties of "Green Ooze" (Ibid.) pg. 4-5

28. Dahmer, Jeffery. Wikipedia (http://en.wikipedia.org/wiki/Jeffery_Dahmer) pg. 1-3

29. Cult of Voodoo (http://www.eaec.org/cults/voodoo.htm) pg. 1-4

30. Ibid. pg. 1-4

31. Ibid. pg. 1-4

32. Ibid. pg. 1-4

33. Ibid. pg. 1-4

34. Gonzales-Wippler, Migene. *The Santeria Experience*, 1982; Thompson, R. F. *Flash of the Spirit*, 1981

35. Religion News Blog. Regarding Santeria (http://www.religionnewsblog.com/17085/Santeria-leader-fights-animal-sacrifice-ban) pg. 1-4

36. Ibid. pg. 1-4

37. Ibid. pg. 1-4

38. Ibid. pg. 1-4

39. PaloMayombe (http://www.PaloMayombe.net) pg. 1-4

40. Ibid. pg. 1-2

41. The Seven African Powers (Ibid.) pg. 1-4

42. Wicca, Pagan Institute Report (http://paganinstitute.org/PIR/animal_sacrifice.shtml) pg. 1-9, *Dictionary of World Religions*. 1997 (Wicca Oxford University Press, Oxford, NY) pg. 1040

43. Cunningham, Scott. *The Complete Book of Oils and Brews*. 1996 pg. 204; Bowker, John. *The Oxford Dictionary of World Religions*. 1997 (Oxford University Press,Oxford, NY) pg.1040

44. Cunningham, Scott. *The Complete Book of Oils and Brews*. 1997. pg. 204

45. Regarding bloodletting. The Pagan Institute Report (http://paganinstitute.org/PIR/animal_sacrifice.shtml)

46. Satanism (http://en.wikipedia.org/wiki/Satanism) pg. 1-7; Satanism (http://www.religioustolerance.org/satanis4htm); Satanism (www.religousfacts.com/satanism); Satanism (altreligion.about.com/od/beliefsandcreeds/tp_satanic_sins.htm)

47. LeVey, Anton. *SatanicBible* (http://en.wikipedia.org,/wiki/The_Satanic_Bible) pg. 1-2)

48. Ibid. pg. 1-2

Chapter Five

49. Big Foot (http://www.unknown-creatures.com/Big Foot.html) pg. 1-3; Sioux name for Big Foot, Big Foot Field Researchers Organization (www.bfro.net)

50. Number of Sightings (Ibid.)

51. Cryptids (http://www.unknown-creatures.com/Bigfoot.html) pg. 1-3

52. Ibid. pg 1-3

53. Chupacabra (www.itsnature.org/legendary-creatures/chupacabra); Phylis Canion,Texas ranch owner, 2007 (http://www.history.com/shows/monsterquest/videos); Chupacabra (http://en.wikipedia.org/wiki/Chupacabra) pg. 2

54. Ibid. pg. 1-3

55. Ibid. pg. 1-3

56. Ibid. pg. 1-3

57. Ibid. pg. 1-3

58. Ibid. pg. 1-3

59. Ibid. pg. 1-3

60. Skunk Ape (http://en.wikipedia.org/wiki/Skunk_ ape.html) pg. 1-3; Skunk Ape (http://www.newanimal.org/gmonkey.html) pg. 1

61. Ibid. pg. 1-3

62. Cadborosaurus (http://www.bcscc.ca/cadborosaurus. html); Cadborosaurus willsi (http:// en.wikipedia.org/wiki/ Cadborosaurus_willsi) pg. 2

63. Ibid. pg. 2

64. Ibid. pg. 2

65. Murphysboro Mud Monster (www.un known creatures.com/ murphysboro-mud-monster.html) pg. 1-3

66. Ibid. pg. 1-3

67. Loveland Frog (http://www.unknown-creatures.com/loveland-frog.html) pg. 1-3

68. Ibid. pg. 1-2

69. Lizardman (http://www.abovetopsecret.com/forum/ thread111225/) pg. 1

70. Lizardman (http://www.unknowncreatures.comlizard-man. html)

71. Lizardman (http://unknownexplorers.com/sclizardman.php) pg. 1-2

72. Ibid. pg. 1-2

73. Ibid. pg. 1-2

74. Dover Demon (http://www.unknown-creatures.com/dover-demon.htmlpg.1-3)

75. Skin Walkers (http://en.wikipedia.org/wiki/skin-walker) pg. 1-2; Skin Walkers (http://navajolegends.org/navajo-skinwalker-legend); (www.rense.com/general77/skin.html)

76. Ibid.

77. Ibid.

78. Anasazi (http://On line Utah.com/history of the Anasazi Indians.utah); Anasazi (http://www.beautifulplacestovisit.com/ up-content/uploads/2011/07/Anasazi_ruins)

79. EbuGogo (http://www.Floresgirl.com/ebu-gogo-legend. html); EbuGogo (http://natural plane.blogspot.com/2010/08/ legendary-humanoids-ebu-gogo-flores.html) pg. 1-6; EbuGogo (http://en.wikipedia.org/wiki/Ebu_Gogo) pg. 1

80. Ibid. pg. 1-6

81. Leed's Devil. The New Jersy. Historical Society, 52 Parks Place, Newark, NJ 07102 (http://www.jersey .org/history/legend-jersey devil.html)

82. Ibid.

83. Ibid. Leed's Devil (http:// www.unknowncreatures.com/jersey-devil.html)

84. Ibid.

85. Mothman (http://www.Monstropedia.org/index.php?title=mothman); Mothman, (http://www.unknown-creatures.com/mothman.html) pg. 1-3

86. Ibid. pg. 1-3

87. The Silver Bridge Collapse (Ibid.) pg. 1-3; Silver Bridge Collapse, Transportation Research Board of National Academies (http://trib.org/view.aspx?id=38760)

88. Batsquash (http://www.unknowncreatures.com/batsquash.html) pg. 1-4; Batsquash (http://www.unexplainedmysteries.com/column.php/id=150840)

89. Aswang (http://mythicalcreaturesguide/page/Aswang); Aswang (http://wikipedia.org/wiki/Aswang) pg. 1-2

90. Ibid. pg. 1-2

91. Rakshasa (http://www.mythfolklore.net/india/encyclopedia/rakshasa.html; Rakshasa (http://wikipedia.org/wiki/Rakshasa) pg. 1-6

92. Ibid. pg. 1-6

93. Snallygaster (http://www.unknown-creatures.com/snallyGaster.html) pg. 1-3

94. Ibid. pg. 1-3

95. Springheel Jack (http://www.unknowncreatures.com/springheel-jack.html) pg. 1-4

96. Ibid. pg. 1-4

[Epilogue

Recently, I was asked by a friend:

"What do you hope to gain by the writing of this book? Will it change some of the goings on?"

I have had to ponder this, because writing this book will not stop the death ships, at least not right away. However, I do believe that evil practices eventually come to an end when the evil doers are confronted by the victims or their survivors. The public must rise up and say: "No more!", "No more of this hideous injustice!"

The Regatta Morte is gradually being defeated, even as we speak, for that very reason. Why, you might ask, hasn't our Father simply put an end to this evil? Here on Earth, we tend to see our Father as omnipotent, as God, and that is not the case. We have a Universal Creator, who is over us all. On Parutia, Father is in human form as we are. He was given the task of bringing all of us into the physical world, and helping us to grow. However, his efforts have often been thwarted by The Darkness. It was The Darkness that set these Death Ships, or the "Regatta Morte," into motion. Father has to obey all of the laws that exist in that solar system, and beyond. There is an Intergalactic Council that sees that these laws are upheld. Father is a member of the council, but as he has said to me, that does not mean that he can get anything he may want. From what I have been told, over 1,000 members represent 80 planets in this council. Had our Father attempted to militarily do away with these ships, our one planet, Parutia, and probably our Earth as well, would have no doubt been destroyed—not by the Council, but by those worlds who participate in running these death ships. The odds were very much stacked against us at that time. Remember, also, that this practice was spawned as a way of getting a rare ore that was, and is, needed to provide energy to many planets. Human souls have been used as partial payment for this ore. As I have stated in this book, these souls are taken to mining colonies and placed into strong genetically modified bodies and are used as workers in these mines. This is not the most evil part of the story! The regatta earned it's name because the people who are kidnapped are not just humanely killed. They are tortured to death in hideous, sick ways. Now that this is out in the open, people of the fifth dimension are calling for an end to this practice and other means of obtaining this ore are being worked out. It is long overdue, and it is my sincere hope that the end to this practice will come in my life time.

Please do not allow these truths to derail your desire to awaken! Having read this book, you now know more about who we are and where we are from than other enlightened people who have gone before. Use this knowledge wisely! Pray and meditate, meditate and pray! Become involved in your communities and be there to help your brothers and sisters whenever it is possible. Our lives here must end, and we will return home to our Father and our homeland. Our souls are immortal, yet we shall endure. Let us strive to be the kind of people that our Father wishes us to be: generous, caring, courageous and loving. We shall return home as one: the brotherhood of man.

Notes